I0054303

OPTIONS TRADING FOR BEGINNERS

A Crash Course in Simple Ready-to-Use Strategies to Create Your Passive Income Fortune by Investing in Forex and the Stock Market

By

Benjamin White

TABLE OF CONTENTS

INTRODUCTION

The history of human beings has been mostly the history of slavery. By this, I mean that Man, throughout history, has been a slave: a physical slave, a mental slave, or a financial slave.

A physical slave when Roman empires existed, ships leaving the African continent, shackles, galleys, plantations.

A mental slave when he has been subject to the control of governments, states, feudal lords, and various institutions that have tamed and domesticated him so that others could carry out their agendas.

And a financial slave, which is the subtlest form of slavery that exists, when you apparently enjoy the income you receive, but you are dispossessed of that money in various ways wisely orchestrated by the elites (among which you do not include yourself, of course): rates that they are created because yes, abusive taxes, bank interests, penalties for late payment, debts (other person!) that you have to pay (and that no matter how much you pay, you always owe), etc.

There may be people who do not share this approach, but I remember that, as someone said, there is no higher jail than that in which the bars are not seen. To tame the masses, you have to convince them that they are free.

Lately, in the most recent decades, everything has been

changing. There is a revolution of consciousness that operates on many levels: personal, spiritual, social, political, environmental, and also, of course, financial.

In this last field, let's say that there are people who are beginning to realize that, perhaps, no matter how hard they work, they never have anything. That others take everything and that one, go to God! It is getting worse.

So they begin to take the reins of their lives and decide what to do at all times (and for the future), regardless of what they have always done or what they have always been told. They begin, say, to be free (oh!!!, a beautiful word, we start to enter into the matter).

Financially and economically speaking, passive income has much to say here. In the next chapter, we will see precisely what they consist of, but for now, you should know that they have a lot to do with words such as independence, freedom, comfort, fluency, self-responsibility, income, etc.

If you resonate with this, we can continue together. If you are afraid of these words, perhaps it would be better if you return to your comfort zone (we all have one, and very nice, as the name implies).

In recent decades, the books of Robert Kiyosaki have become popular, which have titles whose words include those of comfortable retreat, money flow, a conspiracy of the precious, rich child, smart child, etc. etc. And it speaks of passive income and of building automated systems that allow obtaining constant flows of income so as not needed to go to another place to work.

In the same vein, Timothy Ferriss wrote *The Four-Hour Work Week*, taking a radical turn to the thinking of many people. The approach is essentially to live longer and work less. That is, admit that it may not be worth spending a lifetime of work to start living when you retire (assuming you can do it, of course). There is the possibility of working less, earning equal or more, and starting to live from now, without postponing it to the ever-uncertain future.

All these approaches revolve around the idea of passive income. A lot has been written about it; it is a trending topic on some websites, but something fundamental, I think, is missing: a complete and exhaustive list with all the variety of existing and possible passive income sources. I have been studying the subject for years and putting into practice several of them, and I have not found any material or publication that includes a full catalog. Then I decided to create it. And I offer it to you today, here, for your enjoyment and, above all, so that if you wish, you can put it into practice.

To want is 'Power', to want is the first step to 'Achievement', so if you want, go ahead!

CHAPTER 1

WHAT IS AN OPTION

Option contracts usually refer to the purchase or sale of certain assets.

An option is a contract between two parties (a buyer and a seller), in which whoever buys the option acquires the right to exercise what the agreement indicates, although he will not have an obligation to do so.

Option contracts commonly refer to the purchase or sale of certain assets, which may be stocks, stock indices, bonds, or others. These contracts also establish that the operation must be carried out on a pre-established date (in the case of the European ones, since those of the US are exercised at any time) and at a fixed price at the time the contract is signed.

To purchase an option to buy or sell it is necessary to make an initial disbursement (called "premium"), whose value depends, fundamentally, on the price that the asset, that is the object of the contract, has on the market, on the variability of that price and of the period of time between the date on which the contract is signed and the date on which it expires.

Call and Put

The options that grant the right to buy are called 'Call', and those that allow the right to sell are called 'Put'. Additionally, it is called European options that can only be exercised on the date of exercise and American options that can be used at any time during the life of the contract.

When the time comes for the buying party to exercise the option, if it does, two situations occur:

Whoever appears as the seller of the option will be obliged to do what the said contract indicates; that is, sell or buy the asset to the counterparty, in case it decides to exercise its right to buy or sell.

Who appears as the option buyer will have the right to buy or sell the asset. However, if it does not suit you, you can refrain from making the transaction.

An option contract usually contains the following specifications:

- *Exercise date:* the expiration date of the right included in the option.
- *Exercise price:* agreed price for the purchase/sale of the asset referred to in the contract (called underlying asset).
- *Option premium or price:* amount paid to the counterparty to acquire the right to buy or sell.
- Rights acquired with the purchase of an

option: they can be *Call* (right of purchase) and *Put* (right of sale).

- **Types of Option:** there may be Europeans, which are only exercised on the date of exercise or American, to be used at any time during the contract. There are, besides, other more complex types of options, the so-called *"Exotic Options."*

In international financial markets, the types of options that are traded on organized exchanges are typically American and European. In Chile, as with futures, there is no stock market for options.

Practical example

Purchase of a call option by an importing company to secure the Euro price on that day.

To better understand the use of options, this example is presented by an importing company that wants to ensure against increases in the price of the Euro.

To do so, you can buy a European call option today that gives you the right to buy a million euros, within three months, at $ 550 per euro. To acquire that right, the company pays $ 2 per euro, that is, the option premium has a cost of $ 2,000,000.

If on the expiration date of the option, the price of the euro in the market is over $ 550 (for example, at $ 560), the company will exercise the option to buy them, as it will only pay $ 550 per euro.

On the contrary, if on that date the market price of the Euro was below $ 550 (for example at $ 530), the company will not exercise the option, since it makes no sense to pay $ 550 per euro when it can be purchased at the market at $ 530; In this case, the option expires without being exercised.

The cash flows are as follows:

Today (April 10, 20XX).

Buy a European call option, which gives you the right to buy USD 1,000,000 to $ 550 on October 10, 20XX, as the value of the premium is 2 and 1,000,000 contracts are purchased (which means that the notional of the agreement is the US $ 1) there is a cash outlay of $ 2,000,000 for that concept ..

Expiration date (October 30, 20XX)

If the Euro is above the exercise price of the option, it would be exercised, and $ 550 per euro will be paid, that is, $ 550,000,000.

Otherwise, the option expires if it is used, and the euros are acquired in the market.

The euros purchased are used to cancel the importation of goods or services:

The following table shows the result of the operation. As can be seen, if on the expiration date of the option contract, the market exchange rate is lower than the exercise price of the call option, the importer will end up paying the market price per euro plus the cost of the premium (in strict rigor, the value of the premium should be updated for the interest that would have been earned if, instead of paying the value of the premium, that money had been deposited); otherwise, the cost of each euro will be equal to the exercise price plus the premium. That is, the importer will have made sure to pay a maximum of $ 552 per euro.

Market exchange rate A	The exercise price of the option	Prima C	Value of the options (1) D = (A - B)	Result of the options (2) E = D - C	Disbursement for purchase of euros (3) F	Total disbursement G = F + C
530	550	2,000,000	0	- 2,000,000	530,000,000	532,000,000
540	550	2,000,000	0	- 2,000,000	540,000,000	542,000,000
550	550	2,000,000	0	- 2,000,000	550,000,000	552,000,000

560	550	2,000,000	10,000,000	8,000,000	550,000,000	552,000,000
570	550	2,000,000	20,000,000	18,000,000	550,000,000	552,000,000
580	550	2,000,000	30,000,000	28,000,000	550,000,000	552,000,000

Notes:

1. On the expiration date, when the price of the euro in the market is lower than the exercise price, the value of the call option will be zero (as it is not appropriate to exercise the purchase right), whereas, if the opposite occurs, the value of the call option will correspond to the difference between those two prices.

2. That result represents how much money was paid or saved by the fact of coverage.

3. Currencies are acquired in the market when it is not optimal to exercise the option, or by exercising the right of purchase when exercising that right is an optimal decision.

Finally, it should be noted that if a forward-type contract with the same delivery price had been used to perform the same coverage, the importer would have ended up always paying $ 550. However, it would not have had the opportunities (which may appear when hedging with call options) to benefit from declines in the market exchange rate. Also note that the operation is much simpler to perform: a premium is paid at the time of purchasing the option and on the expiration date (or at any time before that date if the option were of the American type) at least the price that has been agreed.

How The Options Work

Option operators must understand the complexity that surrounds them. The knowledge of the operation of the options allows operators to make the right decisions and offers them more options when executing a transaction.

Indicators:

- The value of an option consists of several elements that go hand in hand with the "Greeks":
- The price of the guaranteed value
- Expiration
- Implied volatility
- The actual exercise price
- Dividends
- Interest rates

The "Greeks" provide valuable information on risk management and help rebalance the portfolios to achieve the desired exposure (e.g., delta coverage). Each Greek measures the reaction of the portfolios to small changes in an underlying factor, which allows the individual risks to be examined:

- The delta measures the rate of change of the value of an option regarding changes in the price of the underlying asset.

- The gamma measures the rate of change in the delta in relation to the changes suffered by the price of the underlying asset.
- Lambda or elasticity refers to the percentage change in the value of an option compared to the percentage change in the price of the underlying asset, which offers a method of calculating leverage, also known as "indebtedness".
- Theta calculates the sensitivity of the option value over time, a factor known as "temporary wear."
- Vega measures the susceptibility of the option of volatility. Vega measures the value of the option based on the volatility of the underlying asset.
- Rho represents the sensitivity of the value of an option against variations in the interest rate and measures the value of the option based on the risk-free interest rate.

Therefore, the Greeks are reasonably simple to determine if the Black Scholes model (considered the standard option valuation model) is used and is very useful for intraday and derivatives traders. Delta, theta, and vega are useful tools to measure time, price, and volatility. The value of the option is directly affected by maturity and volatility if:

- For a long period before expiration, the value of the purchase and sale option tends to rise. The opposite situation would occur if, for a short period before expiration, the value of the purchase and sale options is prone to a fall.

- If the volatility increases, so will the value of the purchase and sale options, while if the volatility decreases, the value of the purchase and sale options decreases.
- The price of the guaranteed value causes a different effect on the value of the purchase options than on that of the sale options.
- Usually, as the price of the securities increases, so do the current purchase options that correspond to it, increasing its value while the sale options lose value.
- If the price of the value falls, the opposite happens, and the current purchase options usually experience a drop in value while the value of the sale options increases.

A bonus of options

It happens when an operator acquires an option contract and pays an initial amount to the seller of the option contract. The option premium will vary depending on when it was calculated and on which market options its acquisition was made. The premium may be different within the same market based on the following criteria:

What option has been chosen, in-, at-, or out-of-the-money? An in-the-money option will be sold for a higher premium since the contract is already profitable, and the buyer has direct access to the benefits obtained from the contract. Instead, at- or out-of-the-money options can be purchased for a lower premium.

What is the value of the contract over time?

Once an option contract expires, it loses its value. Therefore, it is logical that the longer the validity period, the higher the premium. This is because the deal has additional temporary costs and that more time is available in which the option can be profitable.

What level of volatility does the market have? The premium will be higher if the options market is more volatile as it increases the possibility of obtaining a more significant benefit from the option. The opposite principle applies to the lower volatility that implies a lower premium as the market is considered relatively 'stable'. The volatility of the options market is determined by using different price scales (the long-term, recent, and expected price scales are the required data) to a selection of price volatility models.

The sale and purchase options do not have equivalent values when they reach their mutual ITM, ATM, and OTM exercise price due to the direct and opposite effects caused by their oscillation in irregular distribution curves, which unbalances them.

Exercises - The number of exercises and increments between the exercises are decided on the basis of the change that is applied to the product.

Option valuation models

It is essential to know the differences between historical and implicit volatility when applied for stock market purposes.

Historical volatility calculates the movement rate of the underlying asset in a given period of time in which the standard annual deviation of price changes is given as a percentage. Historical volatility is the retrospective measurement at the date of calculation of the information available on the degree of instability of the underlying asset in a given number of trading days (modifiable period) and during a selected period.

The implied volatility is the future approximation of the stock exchange volume of the underlying asset that measures the expected variation in the standard daily deviation of the asset between the date on which it is calculated and the maturity of the option. When analyzing the value of an option, implied volatility is one of the critical factors that an operator has to consider. To calculate implied volatility, an option valuation model is used, taking into account the cost of the option premium.

There are three types of theoretical valuation models that intraday traders use most frequently as an aid to assess implied volatility. These models are the Black-Scholes, the Bjerksund-Stensland, and the Binomial. With them, the calculation is done using algorithms, usually buy and sell options are used at-the-money or nearest-the-money.

The Black-Scholes model is the most used with European

options (these options may only be executed on the day of expiration).

The Bjerksund — Stensland model is very efficient if applied to US options that can be executed at any time between the acquisition of the contract and its expiration.

The Binomial model is appropriately applied to American, European, and Bermuda options. Bermuda's are a midpoint between European and American companies and can be executed only on certain days of the contract or on the expiration date.

Types of options

There are two main kinds of options:

1. Selling options: A put option is an option contract that gives the owner the right, but not the obligation, to sell a specified amount of an underlying security at a given price within a certain period of time. This is the opposite of a purchase option, which provides the holder with the right to buy shares.

A sale option becomes more valuable as the price of the underlying share depreciates relative to the exercise price. On the contrary, a sale option loses its value as the underlying share appreciates and its maturity approaches.

The value of a sale option decreases with time since the chances of the stock falling below the specified strike price are less and less with time.

2. The purchase options: A call option is an agreement that gives the investor the right, but not the obligation, to buy stocks, bonds, commodities, or other instruments at a specified price within a specific period of time.

A purchase option gives you the right to buy an asset. You get benefits with a purchase option when the underlying asset increases in price. For example, if a share is priced at $ 50 and you buy your purchase option for $ 50, then you have the right to buy that share for $ 50 regardless of its price as long as the time period has not defeated. Even if the stock goes up to $ 100, you still have the right to buy that stock for $ 50.

The underlying asset

Traditionally, most options have been based on shares of publicly traded companies. However, options based on other underlying investments are increasingly common. This includes options based on stock indices, traded funds (ETF), REIT (real estate investment funds), foreign exchange, and raw materials such as agricultural or industrial products. When it comes to stock option contracts, it is essential to keep in mind that they are based on 100 shares of the underlying value.

An exception would be when there are adjustments by the division of shares or mergers. It is also important to remember that the purchase of stock options is entirely different from the purchase of shares. American options can be exercised at any time between the purchase date and the expiration date. European options can only be redeemed on the due date. Most stock options traded on the stock market are American.

Types of Options:

- Options near month in-the-money
- Protective Sale
- Weekly Options
- Mini Options
- Index Options
- Mini Index Options
- Binary Options
- Futures Options
- Weekly Options EN
- E-Mini Options
- ETF Options
- IRA Accounts

Advantages and Disadvantages of Options

The capital market is full of opportunities as well as risks. To increase chances and minimize risks, private investors should steadily expand and improve their repertoire of financial products that they control. An often unjustifiably neglected instrument are options, partly because of false prejudices and partly because of confusion, options are almost always considered as dangerous and highly risky tools for investing or even compared to gambling. But the truth is quite different: Although options can be wrongly traded and invested at high risk, they often also serve as a hedge or offer the opportunity to seize opportunities with little capital. The pros and cons of options must be disclosed, so you too can benefit as an options investor.

The Main Advantages Of Options

If you look at the various options that the capital market offers to private investors, you will quickly discover that all instruments have their advantages and disadvantages. It is the same with options. Hence, it is quite useful to familiarize yourself with the essential benefits of options before your endeavors with them.

The most significant advantage for many investors is the possibility of being able to set prices without any problems. A short sale with stock lending or the opening of an account with a foreign broker is therefore unnecessary. Put options are suitable for earning on falling courses. You can even decide to go "short" by writing options on rising prices (call options), assuming that prices fall. Another popular feature of options is low capital requirements. Due to the nature of the option, which is just a right to buy an underlying asset, an investment can be made with a much smaller capital investment, which would hardly be possible, for example, directly into the underlying asset. So, about a hundred call options on a particular stock are far cheaper than buying the stock itself a hundred times. Closely associated with this benefit is the leverage effect of options. Depending on the features of the option, the value of the option increases or falls disproportionately to the performance of the underlying. This is a potential benefit for the investor, but it can quickly turn into a downside if the investment is negative.

As a buyer and thus an option holder, you only acquire rights but no obligations. The risk is only in the amount of invested capital, a purchase obligation, or similar outcomes in any case.

Disadvantages Of Options

As always, about investments and the capital market, opportunities and risks together form an inseparable pair. It is the same with options. In short, the biggest risk and, therefore, the biggest drawback of options has already been mentioned: the risk of loss, which is much higher for options, albeit in limited amounts, than for direct investments in the underlying.

This sounds complicated, but on closer inspection, it is not, which can be illustrated sufficiently by an example: Suppose a stock X stands at 100 euros, and an investor considers this course too low. He, therefore, buys call options on the underlying X low, for example, 100 euros as the exercise price. In the future, however, the value of the X share falls to 95 euros, and even on the expiration date of its options, the situation has not improved. The options have thus become worthless, and he has lost 100 percent of his invested capital. On the other hand, if he had bought the X share directly, the investor would have lost only 5 percent of his capital. He would have had to do a lot more but could keep the stock long-term and wait for a recovery. Options are riskier because the expected movement must occur in the period up to the expiration date. An investor saves a lot of capital when doing so.

Another disadvantage of options is the *'Bundling'* of the underlying assets. Options are typically sold as contracts where multiple options are bundled. So the purchase of a single option on a share is the exception and only rarely possible. With more expensive stocks, this, in turn, brings with it a need for capital that contradicts the basic idea and strategy of options trading.

The most significant advantages at a glance:

- With options, investors can participate and earn comparatively easily both in rising and falling prices.
- Unlike stocks, investors can issue options or "write" options.
- The capital requirements for options trading are much lower than for direct investments in the corresponding underlying.
- This lower capital investment results in a lever which, of course, becomes an advantage in the case of positive investment.
- As an option owner, you have only acquired rights; it does not follow any obligation to buy or the like.

The most significant disadvantages at a glance:

- If an option remains out of the money until the expiration date, the investor suffers a complete loss.
- The lever, which becomes an advantage on a positive course, has a negative effect to the detriment of the investor.
- Options are bundled sold as contracts and are therefore not always handled as flexibly as shares.

Is there an additional funding option?

A term that haunts time and again through news and social media, without being familiar to all private investors, is the obligation to make additional payments. It is a red cloth for many investors because here, it threatens unlimited loss. At least now, the attention should be one hundred percent, because the unlimited loss is to be understood literally. Theoretically, any loss is possible with an additional funding obligation.

But when trading options, there is, in most cases, no additional funding. Buyers of options, in particular, are not threatened with additional funding. Their risk is limited to the capital required to buy the options, whether put or call options. If an investor chooses falling prices and the price goes up and up, his option is just out of the money and expires on the expiration date. The same applies to investors who have speculated on rising prices: If the price collapses, the option expires on the expiry date; further costs can never arise.

A margin requirement threatens only the issuer, i.e., the seller (also called writer) of options - and that only in an exceptional case: If an issuer offers options on shares that he does not own at this time, he theoretically has an unlimited risk too. Assuming that one share costs 100 euros and the premium for a call option issued is 10 euros, then the writer would make losses for 110.01 euros. If he did not have the stock in his possession but would have to buy it in the event of exercise first, he would later have to buy this at an arbitrarily high price to then pass it to the option buyer for 100 euros. In this case, there would be an unlimited obligation to make additional payments. Especially for beginners, it is recommended either to only resort to the purchase of options or to offer only options on shares that are in their possession. One speaks in such cases of covered calls.

CHAPTER 2

WHY USE THE OPTIONS?

In some cases, the use of options may limit the losses of investment or earn more than by trading inequities directly.

Here are two reasons why some investors opt for options:

- ## The speculation

Speculation can be thought of as a bet on the evolution of the market price of an asset. The advantage of the options is that you can generate capital gains independently regardless of the direction of the stock price. Given the volatility of the options, it is also possible to win when the stock market falls or goes on the spot.

Speculating on options is a very risky operation. Why?

Because by buying an option, the investor must not only correctly determine in which direction the action will evolve but also the amplitude of this fluctuation. And time is running out, and the option has an expiry date!

But why are speculators interested in options if it is so difficult to profit from them? The answer is simple: the leverage effect. When a single contract controls 100 securities, a small change in the price of the underlying considerably increases capital gains.

• *The cover*

Coverage, or *"hedging,"* is another possible use of the options. It works a bit like insurance. You can insure your car or your home, but you can also provide your stock market with the help of options.

Some question the merits of the strategy of hedging options by pointing out that it is unwise to invest if one is not sure of his choices.

However, even though large institutions mostly use hedging strategies, a private investor can take advantage of options to hedge their portfolio.

Imagine, for example, that you want to take advantage of the potential offered by a particular CAC40 company while neutralizing your exposure to the index. Well, the options allow you to do it.

Development Of The Option

Options belong to the group of financial derivatives. These are standardized trading instruments. The price development of basic security is the measure for the later price. In the case of derivatives, equities, indices, currencies, or even the derivatives themselves may form the underlying. When traded on the stock exchange, investors most often encounter derivatives in the form of options or futures. These forms of investment are among the most traded products on the stock market. But, what is it exactly, and how did the option develop until the speculative derivative emerged as the currently valid trading tool?

- Options are traded on the stock exchange
- The option is a variant of the derivative
- Derivatives may be based on different titles
- Basic title is authoritative for the later price

The classic option offers the right to trade a commodity at a price called *the strike price*. Both the acquisition (call) and the sale (put) may be considered. Trading does not constitute an obligation, which means that the trader does not need to buy or sell the stock or any other underlying asset. It is merely a matter of justifying the right to trade a commercial product at the pre-determined price at a later date. To acquire the option, the investor pays the seller, who is also called the *writer*, a *premium*, namely the option price; A call warrant thus includes securitization on the right to buy the underlying asset. If you trade the American variation, you, as a buyer, can exercise your option right at any time until the due date.

On the other hand, you can exercise your right in the European version only on the due date. In most circumstances, investors will only exercise the call or put if the price of the underlying at the time of maturity is above or below the base value. Otherwise, the investor should trade the security at a better price in the market. For Call and Put, there are the following profiles:

- Call: Purchase Option - Right to buy the underlying

asset
- Put: Put option - Right to sell the underlying asset
- Long: Viewpoint Buyer - buyer position
- Short: Viewing Angle Seller - Verkaufspositon

Note: *Buyers* and *Sellers* refer to the option and not to the underlying asset.

The purchase warrant (call): set on rising prices

The above can best be described by way of example: An investor acquires a warrant of purchase from a bank, also known as an issuer, on a Siemens AG security. This has a base price of 109 euros. The option type is American in this case, and the term has been set to six months. The trader thus has the right to demand from the bank the delivery of the share of Siemens AG at the price of 109 euros. If the paper of Siemens AG is now listed at 120 euros after some time, it is worthwhile for the investor to buy the share at the price of 109 euros. However, should the Siemens share fall to 90 euros, it is cheaper for the investor to buy the security on the market. Therefore, he becomes the option right expire and buys the stock directly on the stock exchange.

However, it remains questionable whether this action also brings the investor a profit. The answer to this question depends primarily on how high the option premium was. Put the case, and the buyer paid a premium of five euros on the right to buy the paper by the due date for 109 euros. In the case of options expiration, the trader has at least made a loss of five euros. When making a purchase, however, he only makes a profit when the underlying asset rises above 109 euros plus the premium, i.e., to more than 114 euros. Under such circumstances, investors may be able to profit indefinitely from rising prices through such a warrant. If the price falls, the loss remains limited to the option premium.

How are warrant options different?

Both options, as well as warrants, are financial instruments with which future transactions are carried out. That's what they have in common with futures. Investors act in these transactions, so to speak, on the development of the option or the warrant. Because trade refers to a delimited period, these two derivatives are based on the same principle. The buyer of the call option speculates that the price of the underlying asset will rise within a specified period or until the due date. This puts the trader in the position to buy the underlying at a meager price. The investor makes the actual profit if he immediately resells the underlying asset in a favorably stored case at a higher value. Thus, he can strike the difference of the market value at the beginning of the legal transaction from the value on the due date.

In contrast, the seller of the call option speculates on a falling price. At the same time, he assumes that the buyer of the right does not avail himself of the opportunity to acquire the underlying asset. Thus, the seller earns a profit with the premium and the further retention of the underlying.

Options and Warrants - A Comparison

Options are standardized products. These are traded as contracts on the futures exchange. By contrast, warrants are among the securities. They are issued by the issuers (for example, the banks). However, the issuer does not usually speculate on a falling price. The issuers issues another warrant, which should have a contrary effect. Thus, the bank escapes the event of taking a risk as the price either falls or rises. The bank generates its profits from the commissions it receives for the issued warrants.

Warrant:

- is issued by an issuer who simultaneously sets the price
- the risk of insolvency borne by the dealer
- only long call or long put possible

Option:

- is provided by each market participant
- no risk, as the legal transactions are hedged
- the price is determined by the options exchange such as EUREX
- the conditions are standardized
- everything is possible such as long call, short call, long put, short put as well as combinations thereof

In principle, options and warrants are quite similar: both are forward transactions based on a previously established underlying asset. This value is also often called an underlying. For both variations, underlying of the following financial instruments may be available:

- Shares
- Currencies
- Indices
- Raw Materials
- Bonds
- Futures

Note: Options are highly transparent as their market value is published on the stock exchange every day. By contrast, warrants issued by the issuer have less transparency.

Trading Based on the Acquisition of Rights

The origin of these speculation products can be found in the Netherlands in the 17th century. At that time, the first tulips were bred there. Sometime after its introduction, the tulip became a popular flower in Holland. Eager flower growers set out to grow specific varieties that would bring in a lot of money. More and more interested flower lovers ordered the particular types from the florists, although they had not yet been brought to market. To give their action a firm reason, they paid for the tulips. In return, the florists offered to purchase a certain amount of tulip bulbs at a fixed price on a specific date. This created the basis for the first option.

In principle, the buyers did not want to invest their money at all, but their will was entirely directed to the exercise of the legal business. However, that could change if the tulips had lost significant value by the exercise date. In this case, the flower buyers were still obliged to purchase at the agreed price, and the tulip seller made a deal.

Note: The development of the option meant that the merchant had no choice during the time the options were created. He had to pick up the tulip bulbs at the previously agreed price, whether he wanted it or not. That could mean a huge win or bankruptcy for him.

The exercise right then and now

The development of the option lasted for a long time. In particular, the exercise obligation has changed over the years. In the early days, the buyer had to exercise his acquired right. If he had been authorized to buy 20 tulip bulbs at the price of 200 guilders, he could redeem them on the agreed date of purchase. If the tulips had risen in price, because the species and genus of this variety had suddenly gained in popularity, the dealer benefited from this advantage. He was then able to sell the tulip bulbs with a profit margin of one hundred percent.

If, however, the demand for this variety of tulips has declined in the meantime, then the tulip bulbs might have been only worth half the purchase date. Yet, even if they had not been worth anything, the businessman of the time had a duty to take off the tulips. The flower bulb buyer was not allowed to indicate that he wanted to renounce the trade. He had to pay the agreed amount of money to the florist and take worthless goods home. This circumstance has completely changed to this day. For the current options offered on the market, the investor can decide whether he wants to exercise his right to end the term or not. The investors enjoy these benefits today:

- if the financial product does not perform as desired, the highest possible loss is the risk of losing the option premium
- the default risk is therefore manageable since there is no commercial obligation
- Traders can still benefit from the better prices if they wish

Note: Financial products due to the transfer of a right now offer traders some advantages over other trading opportunities. If you find that your trade is different than you would like, you can now accept the loss of the option premium and let the transaction expire. You can calculate your risks in advance and act accordingly.

Advantages and disadvantages compared to warrants

Options have some advantages over warrants. This is especially true in terms of the risk involved. With both speculative instruments, traders with small capital can also trade through an account. The investor is not obliged to exercise. On the other hand, he can use the fact that the legal transaction has expired. Also, he has the opportunity to sell the financial derivative, in the American variant even before the maturity date.

Therefore, the investor does not necessarily have to have high financial reserves actually to invest in case of need. Options and warrants are tradable without having to buy the underlying asset. However, there is a unique feature in the warrants. These are rarely actually practiced. Its purpose serves above all the speculation on a profit advantage after a resale.

A lever can be used to multiply the profit of an option. However, it should also be noted that the risk of loss also increases if the price does not appreciate in the predicted way. In this case, traders can lose all their capital. The seller can always reap the option premium.

Both derivatives are used as a speculative instrument. On the other hand, they are an excellent way to hedge another position in the portfolio against loss. This is called *hedging.*

The development of the option

An option gives the investor the right to buy or sell a financial product at a predetermined price. He is not affected by the obligation to exercise the law. He can also forfeit it, losing his option premium at the same time. However, since this is his only investment, the risk of suffering a loss can be kept to a minimum. This benefits the calculability of the legal transaction. For these speculative instruments, the due date must be observed at a predetermined date. In the American variant, the product can be ordered at any time, which is only possible at the exercise period in the European form. Investors take less risk when buying or selling the right than when trading in warrants. In the case of warrants, the trader bears primarily the issuer risk, which is significant if the issuing bank suffers insolvency. Investors can disproportionately share in the performance of the underlying by investing in derivatives themselves by using little capital. In percentage terms, the option value reacts more strongly to changes in the price of a commodity than the value of the product itself. This effect is also called *leverage*. However, dealing with the presented derivatives is best recommended for experienced traders. There should be enough knowledge as well as some trading experience since trading on the stock exchange involves risks.

The Importance Of Your Mindset

It's easy to meet with people every day, who think differently from each other.

It is also easy to notice how, among the different mentalities of people, some patterns are evident. And with the word *'mentality'*, I mean the way of thinking or reacting to everyday events and perhaps, in due course, to those unexpected events.

It is said that every head is a world. That every thinking being on this planet perceives its surroundings differently. Well, what each of us sees as reality, is certainly nothing more than the representation of the universe, which our brain manages to make us understand. It's a matter of specific perception.

Now, if our brains interpret the variables of the universe, each in its way - to put it a certain way - then, why do we commonly find that people tend to follow massive patterns of behavior? And worse, ridiculous behavior patterns?

Why does it seem that the more individualistic and independent we preach to be, the more we tend to go in packs together with the other members of our species, towards the first ravine we see?

My criticism today goes against those who do not think for themselves, and instead, let others do it, following others irrationally or blindly.

«Thinking is one of the most difficult tasks of this life. That is why very few people do it. Who does not resolve to cultivate the habit of thinking, loses the greatest pleasure of life. » - Thomas Alva Edison

This is a call to take the reins of our lives, to realize that it is we who define our present and with it our future. To open our eyes to the stupidity that others have imposed on us whose ends are apparent.

Let's not let ourselves be manipulated; let's not let others be those who define our destiny, nor our direction. We don't have to accept that it is the others that move us like puppets. Why should we be the puppets?

There are lots of cases in society, however, and to get into detail, a typical example of this is employment.

What is the job? Employment is a necessary evil.

Approximately 95% of the people who work do not do it because they want, or because they like it. But because it is their turn. Why do they need money, and why their mind is not enough to give themselves a better life, far from orders, strict and absurd rules, and little time to devote to themselves and their loved ones.

Maybe it's all a matter of fear, or perhaps it's cowardice. Be that as it may, and from any point of view, it is absurd.

Why do we seem to have to live our whole lives doing what we don't want ? Because someone else told us that it should be like that. Because we were programmed to accept such inconveniences since we were little without saying a word. Because we fail to think and avail the enormous opportunities on offer all around us.

We are not robots, but sometimes, we look like it.

And regarding work. Just think about how many people have become rich working? ANY!!!

No, the rich - or those called financially free - are those who discover that the essence of life is not in money. You do not worry about money, but living being working for money, it is absurd. And that not making the necessary decisions to achieve effective maintenance is extremely risky.

Leaving my life in the hands of another, it seems risky, in fact.

The world is continually changing. Today, thanks to the new technologies, we have significant advantages at a general level for our lives. However, so much change is generating fear and indecision, so the advances are ahead of the backward.

The victims of change do not realize that life is NOT as before, that opportunities are changing and, therefore, the schemes under which we develop day by day. And, employment is no stranger to this situation.

In the industrial era, it was a great idea to study hard,

graduate, get professional cardboard. Find a good job and take care of it until retirement, and then be old, live off the pension.

However, there are lots of disadvantages to it. And all mainly, because THE WORLD IS CHANGING. But more important than the world is changing, is that people don't realize it. This is critical, obviously.

SO SIMPLE.

Companies now cut staff every so often, do not want to pay pensions, because they involve exaggerated cost overruns (and more in times of "crisis") ... create modalities of contracts in which benefits are evaded and if that were not enough, time of these contracts, when perfect is one year.

The work is little and poorly paid for these days. It is said wisely that employment is slavery, spread over 8 hours a day.

You only get paid when you work, and if that were not enough, if you have a month of vacation a year, it is something exaggeratedly good.

You miss the good times with the family, and you miss raising and educating your children, you miss being with those good friends, ENJOY LIFE.

And so? If I don't work, what do I do to live? It is the question that people immediately throw at me, feeling confused with my premises.

And the answer to this is straightforward.

What did the creator of Coca-Cola do to live? Look for a job?

And Bill Gates, creator of Microsoft?

Robert Kiyosaki?

etc....

All those did something very different from 99% of people. THEY DREAMED WITH A DIFFERENT LIFE.

THEY EVIDENCED A CHANGE OF MENTALITY.

They dared to imagine that all this could be different and that indeed, seeing life from another approach, life could be better.

«Madness is doing the same things, expecting different results» - Albert Einstein.

Now more than ever, it is straightforward to undertake with all the comforts we have, information, communication... among others.

And I don't suggest leaving work right now and starting a business. But if I suggest making my own objective decisions, without prejudice to external interference, and giving high priority to the important, over the urgent.

All changes take time, and improving our quality of life will not happen overnight. However, to get from one city to another, at least I need to get in my car, and then start.

So ... why not start today with our path? Why not today, why not now?

Why not forget all those stupid prejudices that our society has injected into our minds by all means?

Why not have deaf ears before the crisis and other hoaxes?

For fear? Or maybe because of cowardice?

It is time to leave us with childish arguments and face our destiny. Face our problems and know exactly what we want for our lives. Take the right path, and fight to achieve our dreams.

How hard can it be?

Or rather... how difficult have they told you it is?

But... the same... some entrepreneurs still need SLAVES.

In your hands and head is there, choose the life you want.

Emotions vs. Facts and Strategies

The conflict between these two concepts is the key to the human psyche and the heart of our customers. But how and, more importantly, in what relationship should facts and emotions stand? Antoine de Saint-Exupéry gives us a famous clue: "If you want to build a ship, do not call the men to fetch wood, but teach them the yearning for the wide sea." The rest is easier.

Facts are naturally provable facts. Thus, to a certain extent, price, performance, and various other factors can be compared. So we are moving at this point on the rational level. For decision-making, whether consciously or unconsciously, many emotional criteria are added.

Studies conclude that 70% of buying decisions are made on the emotional level. Even the rational motivations, which account for only 30% of this decision-making, are not entirely free from psychological factors.

The reason is that we conclude transactions, daily necessities, or capital goods because the performance - even the illusion of it - is worth more than the monetary equivalent. The customer sometimes has to be brought to this realization first. To specifically address this fundamental emotional level, one aspect of marketing has become increasingly important for some time now: so-called *neuro-marketing*. This science has recognized that in marketing strategies, occupying emotion fields is more important than general design features of the performance offered. A purchase decision can, therefore, also be described as an *"emotional benefit assessment."*

The combination of picture and sound

The trick is now to extract the core message of service and then accurately transport it to the emotional center of the target group. With media in picture and sound, you can achieve the desired effect with professional advice and implementation, even on topics that are not emotionally tainted at first glance, such as spare parts for the industry. Which plant manager does not need reliability, high quality, reliability, and - as a result - after gaining their prestige? A skillful mix of media turns your need into a need, yours, and, hopefully, yours as well.

So far, I have not been able to determine a gender-specific discrepancy regarding emotional response. However, specific topics are more male or female. So a few months ago, I had a conversation with a good friend, who regularly travels in the areas of airplanes named by me as a show-off class because of above-average professional success. He was seriously concerned that his neighbor on the last trip was wearing a much more expensive watch than himself. The conversation ended with the remark that I would not be able to recapture the last 15 wasted minutes of my life.

Conversely, in a cosmetics shop, I involuntarily took care of the amusement of my teenage daughter, because, following the advice of a trained shop assistant, her overpriced product would "make my beautiful eyes stand out even better ..." happy and with the purchase made, leave the action. How could that only happen to me...

Be More Productive Not Busier

I do not have the time. I am too busy. How often do you hear these two little sentences every day? Far too much, anyway. And honestly, you never achieve exceptional results when it is you who say them, these sentences. So stop being busy and be productive, to accomplish more things, get tangible results, and have the time to entertain yourself!

Perhaps you should make a list of things you absolutely must do today. And the important word of this sentence is *absolute*. The problem with this kind of list is that it never ends if you do not select what is essential - you can add tasks to the shovel and end up spending so much time building this list that we do not even do one. You will understand, this is not the right solution. You should never have to go over 8 points, and again, if you go over five, make sure it's essential. The list should not include things that everyone does (shopping, going to class), but specific points that bring you closer to your goal: read a chapter of a manual, establish a plan for your next presentation, etc.

Learn to do only one thing at a time: yes, being multi-tasking is a talent. But do not overdo it! When you think about it, multi-tasking is efficient when you know how to brush your teeth while you read the newspaper, it saves time.

On the other hand, for actions that require understanding and reflection, it is better to do one thing at a time. When you do something, do not do anything else at the same time. If you think of something else, write it down on a post-it and try not to think about it until the end of your activity. Then, you will resume the post-it and think about your ideas, but not while you focus on a specific action.

Finally, you can keep a productivity log. It seems like extra work, and it is, or at least it will be until you're used to it, and it's a handy tool. So what should you write in your journal? First, list your objectives: those of your life or only of your year, whatever, but you need long-term goals. Then, each morning, write down your list of things that need to be done. Tell them how it went: did you finish everything? How did you feel working? Was it a chore, or was it rather pleasant? Look for trends: times of the day when you feel more productive, the company of some people that can be beneficial or harmful. Finally, you will know exactly how you operate. And you will not need any more general advice because you will know exactly what you need to do or avoid. You will become quite good at *prioritizing*.

Set Your Goals

Peng! Set goals - and the rocket goes off! I used to be so naive when I defined the following formulation:

I was convinced that I had set a strong goal for myself or our company. It was just a vague declaration of intent.

At that time, I had done a lot of wrongs. Today, I know that the achievement of goals begins with the right objective.

This foundation must be strong and clean. Otherwise, success may be nipped in the bud.

How to set your goals so that you have the best foundation for your success is outlined in this section of this chapter. Here I have put together five principles that I apply when I set a new goal.

1. Set your goal with the SMART formula

When I ask others if they have goals, I often hear spontaneously, "Of course, I have goals!". If I drill something, it often turns out that it is only vague wishful thinking - as in my previous example.

Maybe you already know the SMART formula. However, many people don't know anything about it; let alone define their goals.

That is fatal! Because precise goal formulation is just as important as the input of exact target coordinates in a navigation system.

The SMART formula is quite simple:

- Write (if possible only) a sentence in the present-day form with your very concrete, own goal formulation (Show specific).
- In this formula, you need a measure to check that you have reached your goal (M as measurable - e.g., not "a lot of money," but "100,000 €").
- The target should electrify and attract you (A how

attractive).

- Also, the goal should indeed be high, but reachable (R as realistic).
- Most importantly, you include a date in your goal formulation until when you will reach the goal (T as scheduled).

Check your goal formulation for the aspects mentioned above; then, you have an essential foundation to reach your goal.

2. Find a strong why when you set a goal for yourself

The more significant and more challenging your goal, the more critical it is that your motivation, your why for the goal, is crystal clear and strong. Especially under challenging phases and hurdles - which always exist - you need it. Otherwise, you fold in quickly and give up.

I have experienced it several times that I had set myself an "empty goal" with a weak *why*. One that I may have thought that I must "achieve" or was somewhat foreign and did not come from myself.

Think in detail and in peace about why you want to reach the goal. This inner power is critical! Make a note of everything that comes to your mind. I use my success journal.

Also, very important is that your goal is in line with your

values. It makes sense, therefore, that you know your values exactly. Because the more your goal is carried by one of your values, the more intrinsic motivation you have.

If you want to get to the core of your motivation, it can help if you repeat the question of why several times by asking a new why question for your answer.

For example, you have set the goal:

"On 31.12.2019, I have saved € 50,000 on my time deposit account."

Why do I want to reach the goal?

"Because I want to fulfill the dream of a camper."

Why do I want to fulfill this dream?

"Because I need to be able to travel independently."

Why is it essential for me to travel independently?

"Because freedom and self-determination are my most important values."

By doing this, you can better understand your intrinsic motivation.

In this example, you could then unite motorhome and freedom in your why, which emotionally charges you much more.

3. Connect your goal with a visual anchor

Your subconscious mind is your most important ally for your success. Since it works through images and emotions, you should give it such signals so it can support you.

Therefore, we always create or seek a powerful visual motive when setting a goal. It works as a great stimulant for the subconscious mind to support you.

If you have formulated a strong why for your goal, you may automatically feel an emotional inner image within you. Try to make it more visible.

It's not about the target visualization that should accompany you on the way to your destination, but rather about the "cover picture" of your target story. It should serve as a simple, memorable anchor that you always have ready to call, that keeps you pushing harder for your goal.

Be inspired and search the Internet or magazines for motives that resonate with your goal. Of course, you can also let it appear in your mind's eye. However, I like it when I can print a motive together with the goal formulation or save it on the phone or as a wallpaper. So I have it always present in mind.

4. Set goals with the right time horizon

I'm not a fan of target planning with daily, weekly, monthly, and yearly goals. So I do not think about what I want to achieve in a given time, but set a goal and think about when I can reach it.

These are usually the goals that I aim for in a period of two to six months - rarely even more. Of course, this can vary individually and from one goal to the next.

- When I set a goal, I first check it with the following two questions:
- Can I see what specific actions I can / must do today to reach my goal?
- Can I effectively sense the impact of these actions on my goal?

So I can tell if the size of the target fits, if the chosen period is right, and if I need to adjust something, for example, by breaking down the target again.

I tend to advise you on shorter goals. So you automatically get more "train on the chain." You see much more clearly what you have to do, see the effects more directly, and have to accelerate.

On the other hand, if your goal is still a long way off, you may be stuck with irrelevance forever, because "there is still so much time left." Then you may have to shout (too) for a long time, oppress yourself to extraordinary deeds and later forfeit.

5. Commit yourself to your goals

If you set yourself a new goal, you should nail yourself to it so that you can not quickly row back or give up.

I recommend three things:

- Consider a reward for the case of success.

- Make punishment for you if you can not do it.
- Tell others about your goal and the first two points.

You should celebrate success and reward yourself when you reach your goal! So think about how you'll reward yourself if you can do it. This is very important! You may also be able to use the mental image of the reward as a visual anchor. I do that often.

It's just as essential that you do not elude the punishment you set in the event of failure!

How hard you want to be, you have to decide for yourself. When defining a punishment, you should realize that you have to! Pull it through consistently. Otherwise, you'll lose your face in front of you! If you - as recommended - have initiated others, it will be much harder for you to seek escape.

Therefore, tell others about your destination, preferably several people. And also, what punishment you have considered in the event of failure. Ask these people to ask you about it regularly and to specifically discuss the target date if you have reached your goal.

Be aware that your success begins with the right purpose. In the past, I often did not achieve goals because I did not know the connections and therefore lacked this stable foundation.

The five principles described here will also help you to create the right base on which to achieve your goals.

Stay tuned! Your way is the goal!

More Sleep

It's six hours for Elon Musk, five to six for Richard Branson, and only four for Marissa Mayer at Yahoo times: The nights of tech entrepreneurs are short, sleep is almost nonexistent in the daily routines. Work rules of life.

The short night has become a figurehead for workaholics. Polyphasic sleep patterns describe a phenomenon in which people nod for a short section several times a day and forego the classic eight hours. The " Five-AM-Club " brings together people who want to start the working day as early as possible to get rid of essential things in the morning.

What the two phenomena promise: maximum productivity with little sleep or getting up early. You could say that fatigue has become socially acceptable. Because who is tired, he must have worked hard. Anyone who stays awake at night struggles with showing commitment to his job. However, anyone who goes to bed early or spends more than eight hours in bed is considered lethargic, sometimes even lazy. Sleep is overrated, of course.

The mystification of sleep deprivation is not explained. Anyone who studies scientific research realizes that sleep, as time-consuming as it may be, certainly makes sense. The body needs the time of rest; at night, energy is drawn for the new day. Lack of sleep has been shown to reduce attention spans, memory retention, and response time.

Sleep is important for performance

As early as 1996, researchers June Pilcher and John Huffcutt found out in a meta-study that sleep deprivation severely impairs the ability to function. For their study, the researchers evaluated the data of 1,932 people out of 143 study coefficients. Above all, the mood of a person suffers from permanently short nights - perhaps this explains the "terrible depths" and the "relentless stress" that Elon Musk described on Twitter in the middle of the year. The cognitive performance also decreases, even more than motor skills. Recent studies confirm the results.

Of course, such meta-studies can not reflect the individual requirements of the individual. Even though lack of sleep can cause problems, one night does not have to be eight hours for us to recover. What counts is the balance between sleep and wakefulness, also called *homeostasis*. In simple terms, we can only sleep if we are awake long enough. Usually, the optimal waking phase is 16 hours. It can also be shorter or longer, depending on the individual.

If we stay awake much longer, the sleep pressure increases. This is usually not a problem because we can go to bed earlier the next day. However, those who only go to bed at one o'clock in the morning and get up five hours later do not only experience short-term but also long-term adverse effects. In chronic sleep deprivation, overweight and diabetes threaten.

The Internal Clock - for whose research scientists were awarded the Nobel Prize for Medicine in December 2017 - also plays a role here. She determines if we'd instead get up early or be late. If it gets out of balance, it can cause problems. Anyone who has to get up early every day, even though he is a late-sleeper, suffers from a kind of chronic jet lag. This is what researcher Till Roenneberg found out in his *"Munich Chronotype Study 2006".*

If we always rebel against our internal clock, perhaps because we want to belong to the Five-AM club, it can lead to illnesses. Shift workers have a higher risk of heart disease and cancer. Roenneberg has also found that people who do not follow their internal clock smoke more often - even if the correlation is not clear.

The perfect sleep rhythm does not exist

The big problem: there is no guideline for the internal clock. Everybody is ticking differently. An experiment from the 1960s proves this: In Andechser Bunker, subjects spent up to four weeks at a stretch - without sun, without watches. Researchers at the Max Planck Institute wanted to use this method to find out whether the daily routine is controlled by the sun or by the organism. The result: "All day-periodic processes observable under natural conditions are retained," wrote researcher Jürgen Aschoff in 1981. However, the processes shifted: The rhythm looked a little different for each subject; for many, it went beyond 24 hours. Historians assume that continuous sleep is not innate but a cultural product.

Perhaps it can also be explained by cultural conditions that tech companies boast of short nights. At a time when work not only means merit but also creates a deeper meaning for many, short nights have become a status symbol. The lack of bed rest seems to serve as a testimony to how much one uses for his cause: See how hard I toil, I even renounce to sleep for it!

Fortunately, there are always people who are embracing such trends. For example, Microsoft founder Bill Gates says he needs seven hours of sleep a night to be creative. Facebook CEO Mark Zuckerberg states that he has never been an early riser. In the early days of the social network, he is often not supposed to have entered the office before 10.30. And for Amazon boss, Jeff Bezos eight hours of sleep make a big difference. "I'm trying to make that a priority," he once told Thrive Global. "For me, that's the amount to energize me."

The Importance Of A Long-Term Vision

Let's talk about the influence of your perception of the world on your behavior and especially the "temporal" understanding of the world. Let me explain: most of the time, we are in *"short-term perception"* mode. When we decide to make a pizza to eat, we will say that we are in this mode of perception, we use our short-term vision. You can have an excellent reason to eat this pizza (it's okay, no time to prepare something else...) However, with a concept of the medium / long term, you would tend to limit consumption.

It's not a judgment, just an observation. If you become aware when you eat this pizza that in one hour, you will have a big hit, due to the drop in hypoglycemia that will cause its consumption (medium-term vision), that you eat a food that does not bring anything positive to your body and that it is likely to deteriorate in the long term (weight gain, increased risk of disease...) so this pizza will be immediately less attractive.

It often takes a violent shock for the man to realize that he is bullshitting (diseases, accidents, trauma...). It is usually after this first ring of alarm that he will pay particular attention to those little things that are important in the long-term. In this example, the food, since this is a field that can quickly be disabling (your physical and mental shape depends on it). Do not fall into the trap of ease at all costs, and it is often the best way to complicate things for the future.

Let's go back to the original subject. Here I took the example of food, but the principle can apply to many other areas.

If you are on this personal development, I certainly do not need to remind you how important it is to have at least a small idea of what you want to become in the medium and long term if you wish to achieve something essential or enjoy every experience of life thoroughly.

Here are some areas in which it seems to be interesting to apply the principle of long-term vision:

Your future: the importance of having values and setting goals. Also, understand that you can only progress step by step and that you need to establish a set of objectives to make each step a reality. Many men give up when they find that the path is long between the starting line and where they want to reach on arrival. Americans use an expression that seems perfectly suited to the "baby steps" situation. Like a baby who walks on all fours and who will eventually become an adult capable of running the Paris Marathon in 45 minutes. You have to know how to take time and not focus on instant results. Rome wasn't built in a day, after all!

Your diet: Socrates already said, "Let your food be your medicine and your medicine your food. "The junk food from time to time in front of a good football game or the last Sofia Coppola is excellent, but it is certainly not sustainable hygiene in the long run. The body is a machine that requires constant maintenance to function properly. The trap is to think you can eat, move, and reproduce its excesses of youth by believing that you will pass through the cracks. Think again, even the Mona Lisa is suffering the ravages of time, and you will not be the exception that confirms the rule. Take the lead and consider that this is also part of your personal development. Be Ready!!!

Your Seductive Ability: When you discover seduction

sites and communities, you are always happy to swallow tons and tons of books on techniques/tips and tricks to chopper more. Again, this is the simplest, and it brings the most instant satisfaction. But it is a work on the bottom that will be the most exciting and rewarding in definitive. If we speak of "inner game," it is not a coincidence. It makes sense to dig deeper in this area than to get stuck on technical issues "and if she tells me that, and if she does that ...". This will allow you to make concrete progress in the long term, and the rest will quickly lose its importance.

You have understood the principle, be careful not to see either only in the long run. You have to know how to stay connected to the present and enjoy the small, immediate pleasures all the same; it's equally important!

Investor vs. Gambler

At very high risk, completely uncontrollable and unpredictable, yet more and more people are fascinated by the possibilities of winning the lottery, online casino, scratch cards, video games. Does pure mania or gambling have any analogy with riskier and more profitable investments?

Similarities between gambling and investments.

The analogies clearly do not stop at the purest marketing: little difference, in substance, passes between the tissue and the footballer who promise you lavish gains by sitting at the virtual table of a Texas hold'em game and a banker who reassuringly promises the prodigious multiplication of your money by investing in bonds, small caps shares, etc.

In gambling, a certain sum is put into play and invested in one's fortune. Unlike what many claim, there is no real strategy to win and win over the various Superenalotto, roulette, scratch cards, slot machines. But as much luck is needed when embarking on a high-risk investment: potentially very profitable, but equally prone to the laws of Chaos. The axiom that " there is no 100% secure investment, and as risk decreases, earnings decrease " seems to confirm this initial impression.

The "virtual" dimension of various online casinos find logical parallelism in online trading platforms where a usable interface and the ability to see earnings and losses almost in real-time can lead to forms of compulsiveness and dependency. In the case of online trading, however, it is possible to somehow dampen the obsessive nature (which takes over, especially when you lose) through information, or expert advice.

Moreover, from a purely "human" point of view, the attitude of the gambler and the stock market player is characterized by the need, the desire, the need to feel the thrill of risk, adrenaline accentuated by feeling master of destiny, able to dominate the infinite variables of the law of chaos.

It is therefore essential to know how to identify, both in gambling and on the stock exchange, that value called *"Certain Equivalent,"* which in the case of gambling is relatively simple, in the case of equity investments is more complex and regulated by economic calculation rules defined.

The similarities between these forms of investment are therefore varied, but they mostly relate to more purely psychological and personal than technical factors. This is a vital point of the game.

CHAPTER 3

WHAT IS FOREX

Novice traders may have difficulty understanding how forex trading works and they often wonder if currency trading really works.

This chapter explains in detail the foreign exchange market, commonly known as FOREX.

What is Forex? Definition and Explanation

The forex (Foreign Exchange) is the foreign exchange market, where currency pairs like EURUSD or GBPUSD are traded. Forex is an over-the-counter (OTC) market where investors or speculators buy and sell currency pairs.

Forex is the currency market, and currencies, unlike most other tradable assets, are as economic instruments as economic indicators. If countries were companies, currencies would be their actions.

The basic terms of Forex Trading

Knowledge of the language of forex brokers will not make you a great trader, but it will help you understand the data and information needed to become one.

Here are the most important terms in forex trading:

- Currency pairs

- Forex Quote
- Pips
- The spread
- The margin
- Forex Financial Leverage
- The swap
- The lot or the size of the contract
- CFDs
- Forex platforms

Any investor who wishes to engage in currency trading must understand what *forex* is and the basic conditions of this market. Testing *forex* trading on a demo account is a way to learn and better understand forex.

Forex quotes

The currency pair is a crucial concept for the basis of forex trading. For example, the EUR / USD pair. The Euro is called the base currency. The US dollar is called the listed currency. The valuation of the base currency against the listed one gives us the forex quotation.

If we look at the EURUSD currency pairs or other currency pairs on the trading terminal, we see two digits, the bid and ask price. They look like this: EUR / USD 1.1234 / 1.1240. This quotation tells us that we can buy a euro with 1.1240 US dollars because it is the amount requested by the bank - the selling price.

At the same time, we can sell one euro for 1.1234 US

dollars - the offer price. It is easy to see that, in general, a bank buys a currency at a lower rate and sells currency at a slightly higher cost. Banks can do this because they have more influence than brokers.

You cannot simply buy or sell EUR /USD, as you would, for example, with the shares of a company. This is because the currency pair EUR / USD does not exist. Money exists alone, not in pairs. Traders speculate on future price movements without buying currencies.

In forex, profit is realized by the appreciation or devaluation of one currency over another. Suppose you buy euros and sell US dollars (using the currency pair EUR / USD). To make a profit, it is necessary to sell US dollars once the Euro is valued against the Dollar.

There are two things to consider. First, traders never buy or sell physical currency. Secondly, buying and selling take place in all transactions.

Which currencies are traded on forex?

The discussion on how forex works would be incomplete without a review of the most popular activities available to a trader.

The most popular currency pairs in the world - the US dollar, the Euro, the Pound, the Japanese Yen, and the Swiss Franc - are part of a group of significant currency pairs called EURUSD, GBPUSD, USDJPY, and USDCHF.

There are three other conventional currencies in Forex trading: the New Zealand dollar, the Canadian dollar, and the Australian dollar. If they are associated with the US dollar, we get the group of minor currencies: NZDUSD, USDCAD, and AUDUSD.

All other currency pairs in forex trading are generally referred to as "exotic currency pairs" and represent less than 10% of all foreign currency transactions.

Who works in forex?

The most important players in the forex market are:

- Central Banks
- The States
- Other Banks
- Cover Funds
- Investment Funds
- The Brokers
- Professional And Private Investors

Among the forex market participants, central banks have the most significant influence on the formation of exchange rates. A central bank is, in fact, the currency provider for the country in which it operates and is, therefore, the offer on that market. Their decisions have a very significant impact on the price of currency pairs.

Small investors, like retail traders, slightly influence the market, but this influence is visible only due to their large number.

To understand forex, it is important to know that the demand and supply of currencies are continually evolving and you can see the price trend on a tick chart on a trading platform, for example:

Understanding the Forex Market

In the economy, supply and demand design is a model that explains the formation of prices in a free and competitive market. The same principle applies to the foreign exchange market.

Every time you buy a currency, you create more demand in the market, which drives up the price. Similarly, whenever a currency is sold, a surplus of supply is created, which pushes the price of the currency down.

The impact of each purchase and sale on the forex market is directly proportional to the trading volume of each transaction.

The philosophy of price balance is the key to understanding how online currency trading works since all economic events in the world have an impact on the market.

Factors that influence FOREX

Several factors influence the forex market and currency prices:

- Interest rates
- Inflation
- Political, economic events, and natural disasters

- Economic growth rates
- The offer and demand of a currency pair

The online broker industry

The functioning of the currency market could be imagined as an ever-changing ocean. There are many fish in this ocean. From the largest to the smallest, depending on their purchasing power.

There are many important players, such as national banks, multinationals, hedge funds, etc.

There are also medium-sized fish - private investors, companies that need forex to protect themselves from currency risk, etc.

There are even smaller players - online brokers, smaller banks, and small investors.

Most of the above-market operators have direct access to the interbank foreign exchange market. They can do it, simply because they exceed a certain threshold of funds. This means that they can change currency directly without intermediaries.

The smallest player - the plankton of the financial ocean - which floats, trying to survive long enough to grow, is the currency trader, i.e., the individual investor.

The buying power of a trader is generally so insignificant compared to the big fish that he needs a forex broker or a bank that provides a trading account with financial leverage and real market access through a trading platform.

To understand forex, it is essential to know that there is no trading on its own as an individual without a forex broker that makes intermediation.

Forex trading is the activity of buying and selling currencies. Forex trading is carried out for speculative purposes or to hedge the exchange rate risk through a trading platform.

How Is It Analyzed?

The analysis is not only the key to success in trading, an analysis is, to a certain extent, trading itself. It's the only thing that makes currency trading work.

The two main methods of market analysis are *fundamental analysis* and *technical analysis*.

Fundamental analysis is an advanced form of financial audit, only at the national or sometimes global level. It is the oldest form of price forecasting that looks at an economy: the current phase of the cycle, relevant events, future forecasts, and the possible weighted impact on the market.

The fundamental analysis relates with national GDP and unemployment rates, interest rates and export amounts, war, elections, natural disasters, economic progress, etc. Fundamental analysis requires an understanding of the international economy, addresses factors that are not yet taken into account by the forex market, and works for long-term investments and exchanges.

The disadvantage of this type of analysis is the element of uncertainty created by many complex parameters.

Technical analysis is a younger form of market analysis that deals only with two variables: time and price. Both are strictly quantifiable, explained by the market, and are undeniable facts. This is why for many currency traders studying charts works better than doing fundamental analysis.

When drawing support and resistance lines, identifying key levels, applying technical indicators, or comparing candles - you discover what forex trading is without examining the causes of supply and demand.

To simplify, fundamental analysis is an economic detective with elements of future forecasts, while technical analysis is visual price-time archeology combined with statistics.

Winnings favor trained people

The lack of training is the reason why so many novice traders fail before they can even genuinely understand forex trading.

Some people, due to the nature of their business, present forex as a pseudo-scientific gambling attraction that is almost like playing a coin, an attraction that has a better methodology to a certain extent, is more fun, has more prestige and the opportunity to make money very quickly.

As a result of this marketing, newcomers with little or no training expect to make a fortune starting at $ 10, with just a few key clicks. They jump into the market full of hope, and the market hits them hard and empties their pockets. This is neither good nor bad - that's why the market exists. Every time someone closes with a profit, someone else has to close with a loss.

Forex trading is an investment activity available for any trader who has a computer and an internet connection.

Understanding the word *"Trading"* is simple: it is about placing orders on the stock market. Negotiation means an exchange between different investors on the stock exchange, who exchange different financial products.

The word forex is a term that refers to the currency market, on which different investors exchange currencies and other financial assets.

Currency exchange is an everyday activity that takes place every day around the world. Governments do forex; banks do forex; even individuals do forex.

Trade takes place through computer networks among all the world's traders, electronically. The reason why forex is the most liquid market in the world is that it is the most accessible. As a result, the most difficult to manipulate.

How to trade Forex?

The logic of forex trading is simple. A trader buys a currency pair in the hope that its price will increase. The trader sells the currency pair when he thinks the pair will fall.

For example, the EUR is at 1.0895 today. The trader believes that the price of the Euro will increase in the next 24 hours. The merchant makes a purchase order. Tomorrow the Euro is at 1.090, and the trader closes his position with a profit of 5 points. The amount of the gain depends on the size of the trader's contract for this exchange order. The gain can be 50 cents or 50,000 euros, depending on the size of the order.

Looking at this currency investment process in detail, we realize that investing in forex is a little more complicated than ordering.

CFD is a tool that has transformed the financial market into what it has become today. It is a financial instrument that allows you to invest a financial asset, such as currencies, up or down.

The forex trader does not hold the underlying asset, but only collects the difference between the entry price and the exit price of the position. This also allows us to speculate on the decline in currency prices.

After finding his forex broker, choosing his trading account, a trader installs his trading software and finances his account.

Multiple trading tools are now available to traders to start trading forex online. If the trader wants to trade a particular currency pair, such as EUR / USD, or a specific configuration of the market, such as the level of support or resistance, the trader must be prepared for a forex order!

The rush to invest is strongly discouraged, although this may be compatible with individual trading styles or forex market configurations.

Technical or fundamental analysis is crucial for online investments. We can start by analyzing the favorable market conditions for entering the position, the management of the money, the duration of the transaction, an estimate of the volatility for the period, the expected macroeconomic events and, above all, the exit times from a trading position on the forex market. All this reflection must be done before placing the stock market orders.

Once again, ANALYSIS IS THE KEY to forex trading! It is essential in the psychology of the trader and the evolution of the balance of the trading account. It is the equivalent of a business plan for an entrepreneur who wants to start a business. The ability to find, analyze, synthesize all this information is essential for forex trading! Mastering these aspects of trading is what makes the difference between success and failure in online trading.

Once the trading strategy is well defined, the order is made with a simple mouse click on the trader's software. Order is the least important part of foreign exchange trading.

What Are The Advantages Of Forex Trading?

You are in control! You decide where you want to live, when you want to work, and how much you want to work. The word "unemployment" no longer frightens you. And when you are asked what your job is, you answer: I sell and buy money.

The crisis is no longer a threat to you! Why? Because during financial crises, almost all assets follow the same pattern. This is the market trend. While the general public prefers bullish trends, forex traders do not care about market trends - they can operate profitably both upward and downward.

For example, in 2008. Your real estate is depreciated. Some currencies lose their value. All this while crude oil is rising from all-time highs.

If you are an online trader, you know the three golden rules of trading in times of crisis: selling currencies, storing real estate, and buying oil.

Remember: financial speculation is a freedom of the capitalist world.

In a highly capitalized environment, currency trading with CFDs is one of the activities available to proprietary traders against economic tsunamis, earthquakes, and wars. Provided that you know, of course, what you are doing—the most crucial factor for success, of course.

Why invest in forex?

The market is open almost 24 hours a day, five days a week.

Forex is the most liquid market in the world.

Brokerage commissions are lower than in other equity markets.

You can trade forex from home; you need to have a trading account with a forex broker.

Understanding Forex - Conclusion

If this chapter is your first step in learning the basics of forex, don't stop there. Be eager to learn much more, and you will definitely thrive!

To better understand how forex works, we recommend that you open a demo trading account and try it yourself.

CHAPTER 4

FOREX SCAM AND HOW TO RECOGNIZE AND PROTECT YOURSELF

Online trading scams are a reality, even in Europe, where the number of fraud victims in trading is impressive.

In this section, you will learn how to protect yourself from forex trading scams:

- How to choose a serious and reliable trading site?
- How to detect a trading scam?
- What are your options if a forex trading scam occurs?

It is said that the forex scam in online trading will exist as long as the forex market exists.

As the patterns evolve, forex scam sites try to extort your money. But is there a solution to this problem?

Since there will always be a fraud in trading, make sure you don't fall into the trap.

Commercial scammers tend to turn to novice traders, who are desperate for an income or who have not yet practiced enough, and hence the most vulnerable in the market.

The best antidote is knowledge. The best advice we can offer is to learn the fundamentals of the forex market and develop advanced techniques.

Once you have mastered the market, you will no longer be an easy target.

For this reason, we always recommend that you continue your education.

Sometimes, forex scams bear the creator's name, like the Ponzi scheme, developed by Charles Ponzi.

However, one thing is common: forex trading scams often use expressions such as "an investment opportunity that is too good to be true" as a tactic to attract attention and get your funds. Unrealistic promises are often a bait.

That's why when you have no trading experience, and a fraudulent trading site will try to exploit your optimism and your fears.

Nobody wants to lose their money, and this will be a strategy that forex scammers will use to make you an attractive offer that you won't be able to refuse.

Did you know that the forex market is the largest financial market in the world, with over 5 trillion euros traded every day? Not only does it allow central banks and companies to trade with each other, or tourists visiting new destinations, but it also will enable speculators to take advantage of a market that operates 24 hours a day, five days a week.

There has never been an easier time to enter the world forex market. With a single click of a mouse, you can trade on the direction of the Euro, the British Pound, the Japanese Yen, the US dollar, or even the Russian Ruble! There are hundreds of currency pairs to trade from, so you are free to find the ones that interest you the most.

However, while the financial gains of trading on the forex market seem lucrative, it is not considered easy. Having a reliable trading education, a properly funded trading account, and a comprehensive understanding of risk management techniques are essential. Unfortunately, many unscrupulous individuals will try to cheat beginners with forex trading scams.

Traders deceive themselves

Since forex trading carries an exceptionally high risk, losses are inevitable.

Some traders are almost always undercapitalized and subject to the problem of gambling addiction and improper use of leverage.

Any speculator who works without the necessary skills plays effectively against the entire market as a whole, which has almost infinite capital, so it will almost certainly lose its initial investment.

Under-capitalized traders who have no information advantage should understand the different reasons why they think they can beat the market in such a challenging trading environment.

In any case, much of the total number of claims for fraud

presented to brokers occur as a result of a low level of training in trading and market awareness, rather than for genuine scams fore.

It is always easier to blame others as a first choice than to take responsibility for our shortcomings.

If bad traders spent adequate time developing a consolidated trading plan and looking for the right broker rather than complaining about a predictable failure, they could become successful traders much faster.

Most good traders should be able to use almost all trading platforms with any broker and see very few differences in their results - it's that simple.

Once you accept your losses, trade with a studied system, and control the market, it will be much more difficult to fall into a forex scam.

Some Examples To Better Understand

But let's see now what the real cases of forex scam are and how they differ.

1. The scam on the trading site

Although there are, of course, many regulated and reliable brokers, many online trading platforms are scams. Before working with a platform, check its reputation and make sure it is not in the blacklist of your local regulation.

Trading with a safe and reliable tool is fundamental for having a productive and satisfying trading experience.

2. Scam Forex Trading

Although the forex market is a risky market where money can be lost, it cannot be said to be intrinsically a scam market.

When we talk about forex trading scams, we're talking about scams perpetrated by fraudulent trading platforms.

If you practice forex trading with a severe and regulated broker, you will receive adequate training and practice on a demo account, reducing risks to a minimum. It's highly advisable to practice on a demo account first.

3. Scam forex high-frequency trading

High-frequency trading is the high-speed execution of financial transactions using algorithms.

This is an automatic trading category that raises ethical and regulatory issues but is not illegal.

4. Forex scam with robots

Not all trading robots are the same. Trading robots are not a scam in themselves, but many trading sites have made the sale of trading robots a fraud.

This is because they promise their victims, novice traders of course, quick and easy profits.

5. Forex scam with social trading

The social trading, trading or copy, is to replicate the experienced trader's operations.

Although this is a new practice, the risk of loss is not inferior to that of traditional trading.

6. Forex scam with false repayment

The reimbursement fraud is a double sanction imposed on the victims who have already been scammed the first time.

It consists of making believe the possibility of recovering all or part of the funds lost by a fraudulent broker, in exchange for a sum of money, to fall back into the same scam.

These entities are typically bogus banks, fake law firms, or various debt collection companies.

7. Forex phone scam

The regulated entities we usually work with have obtained our data legally. Furthermore, with the GDPR (General Data Protection Regulations), it is possible that we must give our permission to send commercial offers.

But if an entity that we do not know contacts us to offer us an investment, we must be extremely cautious because it is probably a forex scam.

Clues to Identifying a Forex Scam

If we pay attention to the following indicators and signs of a possible forex scam, we will have many more opportunities to avoid it, so keep reading carefully!

1. Trading and training systems without evidence

There are many scammers selling trading systems and training programs.

When you ask them to provide proof of their business history, they avoid the answer.

There are also many traders offering their systems without any service. These traders offer "infallible" trading systems but have no valid proof of their trade history.

Therefore, the best option is usually to access free training programs from regulated and reliable sites.

2. Spam Mail Requiring Personal Information

Scammers can also ask you for personal information, for example, by e-mail:

- Your full name
- Your phone number
- Your address

Don't give your contact details to someone you don't completely trust.

Beware of brokers who do not present a risk warning on their web page and in their marketing material.

Even if they do, read the warnings carefully because the scam is in the details.

Remember → Your data could be disclosed massively and instantaneously.

3. Watch out for great promises

Easy money-making? No way! Don't believe someone who tells you it's easy to make money with a monthly rate of return of 20%. It does not make sense.

Forex and CFD trading takes a long time to be a profitable option.

There is no easy money here. If you invest the time needed to practice and learn to trade correctly, you would have a great source of income. But with work, effort, and above all, with time!

4. Unprecedented

Never work with someone who refuses to give you the necessary information. Whether it's a broker, a trader, a trainer, or a fund manager.

You should always do a quick online check to see if the person or company is legitimate.

As Mr. John Naisbitt once said: "We drown in information, but we lack knowledge."

5. False stories reported by the media

A prevalent form of forex scam is viral news. For example, the story of a child who became famous during the night.

According to New York Magazine, a young man from Queens earned tens of millions of euros thanks to the stock actions he was negotiating during lunch hours at Stuyvesant High School.

What happened was that he never really made those profits, since all his earnings were made on a demo trading account.

How to deal with a forex scam?

Have you been a victim of a forex scam? There are two types of resources, depending on whether or not the company that created you is regulated:

- If the entity is controlled, you can contact the Financial Ombudsman Service or the Financial Services Compensation Scheme (FSCS) if you believe this company has cheated you. This can be done by e-mail or by filling out a form.
- If the institution is not regulated, it is possible to apply to the ordinary courts of the place where the fraud occurred.

Please note that these procedures are free and wary of any entity that promises to release funds lost in exchange for a fee or different registration fees.

We have noticed that there are victims of double fraud with false reimbursements, and therefore, it is advisable to check these sites to find out if the institution in question is authorized to operate.

How to choose a suitable broker

Although trading and scams go hand in hand, fortunately, it is possible to trade without risk in a severe trading site.

To do this, it is necessary to verify two crucial points:

1. Check on the FCA website that your broker is not blacklisted for illegal financial sites.
2. Search for opinions and evaluations online on the broker, as well as correctly read all the information on financial security on the broker's site. The difference between a legitimate and an illegitimate is obvious!

When making these checks, pay particular attention to the spelling of the broker's name: illegal sites often use a name similar to that of a severe and regulated broker, changing only a few letters: it's identity theft.

Identify a forex scam

So, if there is trading, is there a scam? Not necessarily.

There are several regulated and reliable brokers, whose reliability can be verified on the website of the financial regulatory entities.

Trading certainly involves risks, but it is a severe and legal activity whose image is unfortunately obscured by the forex scams carried out by some criminals.

To make sure you don't become a victim of a scam, always use the services of a regulated broker that has positive opinions online and is 100% transparent in its compliance policies.

The fascination with quick and easy money will always be present, so the most important thing to do is to understand what is needed to succeed in forex trading. And for this, the best way is to try a free and risk-free demo account.

CHAPTER 5

RISK & MONEY MANAGEMENT

The profitability of investment must always be related to the risk of capital loss that it makes you take. Above all, this risk must be in line with your investor profile.

For your wealth, good risk management is essential.

Investment solutions that are both profitable and risk-free do not exist. All investment proposals in this direction must be avoided at all costs because the real "risk-free" rate of return is traditionally given by the OAT 10 years of France. And that is currently negative.

Some investments offer a capital guarantee at any time. This is the case, for example, of the Livret A, which reports, net of social security contributions and taxes, 0.75% per year. This is also the case of funds in euros of a life insurance policy, which distributed an average of 1.8% in 2018; however, it takes correct social contributions (17.2%) and the taxation upon withdrawal.

Calculated risk

This attractive remuneration compared to the current level of bond yields, is linked to the better return on investments made in the past. That is why the erosion of euro money yields is slow.

Beyond these levels of expectation of remuneration, any investment necessarily entails a greater or lesser risk of capital loss.

This does not mean that you should avoid taking systematic risks with your investments. The risk must be calculated and match your investor profile because a reasonable risk, in the long run, is paying for your wealth.

The 80-20 strategy

For savvy investors who have time to spare (at least eight years), a strategy known as 80-20 may be relevant.

It consists of placing 80% of their savings on secure assets such as funds in euro life insurance contracts rewarded by Le Revenu and 20% on unsecured products, rather oriented in shares.

Thus, in the long term, the remuneration of the secured party will make up for any loss of value of the risky part. In the long run, your capital is more or less protected, even if the financial markets turn around. And if the markets are on the rise, the overall performance of your assets will be very attractive.

Investors with a more dynamic management profile may increase their share of unsecured assets. The ideal being always to diversify the underlying (equities, real estate, bonds...), maturities, and geographical areas.

Psychological factors often influence investment choices.

Investors are thus characterized as overly optimistic when financial markets are expensive and too pessimistic when they have fallen sharply in these conditions, difficult to perform.

Invest regularly

To limit this, multiply the "entry points" to smooth the risk and avoid buying at the highest. For that, continually invest (every month, for example) on several supports to constitute you an average cost price.

Many life insurance policies also offer tailored management options that take the form of automatic arbitrage. Other equally exciting options limit the loss in the event of a decline in the financial markets.

By combining several of these options between them, you frame your investments and your maximum risk-taking — the guarantee of a serene investment.

CHAPTER 6

FOREX STRATEGY
Why use the Forex strategy?

Perhaps you, too, have heard of the fact that in forex trading, many people lose money. Well, we are certainly not here to deny the evidence, and we want to inform you as honestly as possible; the reality is there for all to see and offers staggering numbers regarding the winning and losing financial operators in the field of forex trading. In recent years, mainly, an unexpected massacre has occurred: about 90% of those who trade in Forex end up losing their capital over a period of time that can vary from 6 months to a year. Only 10% of financial operators succeed in bringing satisfactory results home, in simple terms, to earn well and consistently over time.

But at this point, a question arises: how is it possible that there are such negative statistics on online trading? What is this almost catastrophic fact that seems to leave no hope for those who approach financial products for the first time? From the analyses carried out by the experts, a tendency is clear: in recent years, there has been a boom in memberships in online trading, a real race towards the riches of the financial markets that does not seem to want to stop at anything, but the newcomers are ready to make investments in forex? It just doesn't seem like it, and the most meaningful explanation lies in the fact that you don't use a forex strategy. Let's discover together why using a forex strategy is a guarantee of success, but also the reasons why you can do it too... and immediately!

Free Forex Strategies: Find Them Here!

The forex is made on a scale; there are those who go down, and there are those who go up...

The trivial paraphrase of a famous saying we have given above can help you understand how things are going in trading. The fact that most retail traders lose does not mean that there is no one who scales forex, which means positive prospects for your trading account in terms of profits and profits, which would be unthinkable with any other online activity, but let's try to understand why there are many traders who lose and few who earn.

First of all, it must be pointed out that this boom, known from online trading, has led many people to start trading without any preparation. We are talking about people who are attracted by the earnings prospects that probably, having arrived at online trading thanks to some deceptive advertising, have used their capital as if they were at the racecourse to place a bet on horses. Fortunately, online trading on forex is something else or something that has nothing to do with a bet or any recreational activity.

Investing in the forex market is a severe opportunity that must be exploited professionally through the implementation of STRATEGIES. This is a word that sums up different meanings:

Forex strategy is not tactical: a strategy is a method studied in detail that has been developed to achieve precise objectives along a long-lasting path. A tactic instead is only a technique that is adopted to obtain a result in the short-term that often is not based on particular criteria, so here is that the tactic is similar to a bet.

Investment Plan: strategy in forex also means having a precise investment plan, all based on the capital you have available. The plan must contain monthly and annual objectives, the balance of income and expenses, and the planning of the daily investment activity, including a study on financial assets.

Forex Money Management Strategy: managing investment capital is an aspect of primary importance when doing forex trading. Too many beginners underestimate this aspect, and not by chance do ALL pay the consequences. The investments must, therefore, be weighted and well thought out, and the money must be rationalized for each open position on the market.

Forex "Technical" Strategies: in the last analysis, we must mention that for strategies we also mean the "technical" ones, i.e., those based on the use of technical indicators that are used to study the trend of financial assets on the short and medium-term, which are fundamental for intraday and multiday trading.

The Secret Advantage Of A Strategic Approach To Forex

As you understood from the previous paragraphs, choosing to approach the forex strategically allows you to obtain significant benefits and satisfactory results, but we want to close the discussion on the importance of strategies revealing a small secret that 90% of retail traders who lose money every day ignore or choose to ignore. Learning strategies can take some time and a certain amount of patience, but managing forex trading strategically offers you a little-known advantage that turns out to be decisive: a forex strategy like the ones you have the chance to know here guarantees you the average success in 75% of market positions for two reasons:

These are the same strategies that are used by experts in the sector with the only difference that here they are understandably explained to you without leaving room for empty technicalities that are ultimately only counterproductive and prevent bright and lasting learning over time.

The strategies are all based on the most essential and proven technical and fundamental analysis tools for financial markets. Even the use and understanding of these technical tools will be unaffected because our explanations are geared towards newcomers to the sector; on the other hand, an expert certainly does not need to contact us.

In the field of trading, there is so much misinformation and wrong information that we have decided to make the maximum clarity here by offering free forex strategies for all beginners who are looking for severe earnings methods. If you are not willing to learn and apply strategies with commitment, then forex trading is probably not for you, but if you want to get serious here, you find all the material you need.

Forex Intraday Strategies

In forex trading, there are no rules regarding the duration of the investments, that is the time span along which an open position is maintained. Every trader is free to choose his style without any conditioning, but it is clear that the general tendency is to do daily trading.

Intraday trading has great appeal, which is why among the forex strategies we offer here, intraday strategies have plenty of space and high effectiveness to allow you to make profits daily. But let's go into detail and see what the main types of trading are along with their relative advantages.

Medium And Long-Term Trading

When an open market position remains such for a period exceeding 24 hours, then one can speak of trading in the medium / long term. Many traders prefer this type of investment because it guarantees good margins of success, but for the most part, they are financial operators that have already been tested and experienced, able to cope with sudden changes compared to long-term forecasts and to management positions even for a few months to get dizzying gains.

Trading in the medium and long term is suitable for investors capable of making fundamental macroeconomic analysis. This type of analysis has a very mild impact also on the intraday and concise term forex, but we define fundamental analysis:

With the help of fundamental analysis, traders try to bring out the so-called "substantial value" of the financial product or asset, that is, its intrinsic value. This is a feasible operation for any asset, for the stock, as well as for currency pairs in the forex market and commodities. The fundamental analysis lends itself, in short, to any category of assets on which it is possible to invest in forex or with CFDs.

To better understand what we are talking about, you can simply think of the stock market where, precisely, the shares relating to listed companies are exchanged, the role of fundamental analysis is thus easily identifiable: a structural analysis makes it possible to identify the strength of a company on the market (therefore the value of its shares) going to check what the deficit is and what the profits, and in general, what is the state of health of the company.

More specifically, the task of fundamental analysis is also that of understanding which external and internal factors can influence the value of that company, raw material, or currency. Once comprehended what are the factors that influence the assets, it is straightforward for the traders to understand which information to look for to place prudent and profitable investments based on the excellent information obtained.

Short And Concise Term

Intraday trading or day trading on Forex is undoubtedly the preferred type for all retail traders in the world, and the technique is to open and close positions within a day so that they never stay open for over 24 hours. It is a pleasant and exciting type of investment able to bring to life the sensations of the true trader, but above all to bring daily profits that are directly tangible to the trader, this perhaps explains the success of this type of trading and consequently also of the strategies of Intraday Forex. The intraday trading is much easier to manage than long-term; this makes it suitable even for those traders who do not have a very long experience in the field of Forex. Here is a compendium of features required of a trader to make intraday earnings:

- Stress management skills.
- Knowledge of investment assets.
- Technical analysis of financial markets on charts.
- Knowledge of short-term investment strategies.

Technical Analysis For Intraday Forex Strategies

Analysts call " technical analysis " the study which aims to analyze the price trend of the various financial assets in specific time frames, to understand how to participate in the market in the immediate future. This definition is in itself very fascinating because it reflects reality; technical analysis is a method of analyzing price trends that allows us to know the price trend in the short and medium-term with excellent approximation.

Being able to make a precise and consistent technical analysis means earning in most of the positions that are open to the market. Of course, you can't think that with technical analysis, you automatically earn. Still, without the technical analysis, the assumptions of the investment in the short and very short-term would disappear, and there would be no winning intraday Forex strategy.

Traders from all over the world analyze the market on mathematical and statistical models. Based on technical/graphical indicators, which are widespread, financial operators obtain signals of entry and exit from the market that are always "fresh" and effective in most cases. The data and signals obtained from the price chart analysis tools are useful to understand when to open and close positions in the market and therefore help you save money and maximize profits. TECHNICAL ANALYSIS is ultimately the key to success in investing in Forex.

Forex Scalping Strategies: Fast Trading

If, as we imagine, you are interested in intraday trading, here you can find all the strategies you want, all studied and proven as they are used every day to earn from countless traders even among the most experienced. But if you are a lover of Forex intraday trading, you may also be interested in Scalping, the fastest form of trading there is. If you are looking for Forex scalping strategies here, you can find bread for your teeth; in fact, there are plenty of trading techniques suitable for those who want to act aggressively on the market to attack profit!

CHAPTER 7

STOCK TRADING

Stock trading is one of the highest yielding investments. The fact that many do not dare to bargain on shares is partly due to the lack of information about stock trading. We want to close these information gaps with the following share advisor. Because stock trading requires a knowledge base: we are going to show you what you need to consider when trading stocks and how you can achieve a good return even in low-interest phases.

What are public companies and shares?

The legal basis for shares and stock corporations can be found in the 410 sections of the Stock Corporation Act (AktG). A corporation (AG) divides its share capital into shares. The shares are sold to investors on the stock exchange. Each buyer thus owns a share in the issuing company, which receives financing support through the sale of shares. As a shareholder, shareholders also have a say in important company decisions. Investors exercise this right to participate in the Annual General Meeting. Any shareholder can either participate or instruct a representative to exercise their voting rights.

How do I make profits with stocks?

Shareholders benefit from the dividend paid and from the difference between the buying price and the selling price. A dividend is an amount that the corporation distributes to shareholders as a partial profit. Each share consists of two parts: the so-called *coat* and the *coupon*. The coupon represents the dividend entitlement that most types of shares have. The amount of the dividend will be decided in the Annual General Meeting and depends on the business results of the past year. If a fiscal year does not go well, the payout can be meager, or the company pays no dividends. While the dividend is usually paid once a year, investors can always make a profit by buying and selling stocks.

To achieve price gains

Shares are traded on the stock market. For this purpose, the trading systems of the stock exchanges continuously create selling prices and purchase prices for each share. If an investor buys a paper at a low price and sells it at a higher price sometime later, his profit is in the difference between the buying price and the selling price. This difference is also referred to as the *spread*. However, there are fees for each transaction and taxes on profits that reduce returns. The order fees depend on the custodian account, so it makes sense to perform a detailed custody account comparison before investing in securities trading and to find the custody account that suits your investment type and your requirements.

What do I have to pay for stocks?

At the first issue, i.e., the first issue of shares, the stock corporation and the bank accompanying the IPO determine the price of the shares. After that, the price is decided on the stock market by the principle of supply and demand. The information is either in Euro per piece or as a percentage and is independent of the nominal value of the papers. The sale price for shares is also called the *asking price*, while the bid price is known as the *bid price*. The stock exchange ensures that a fair price is given when trading stocks. The stock exchange receives commissions for the placement work.

Different types of shares

The Stock Corporation Act allows companies to issue various types of shares, as the issuance of shares is also called Initial public offering (IPO). The most important types of shares include:

- No-par value share: represents a share of the capital stock
- Par value share: has a fixed par value
- Ordinary share: is provided with all rights for shareholders
- Preference share: gives the shareholder preferential rights, for example, a higher dividend
- Registered share: belongs to a buyer known to the stock corporation
- Bearer share: belongs to an anonymous owner

The type of share does not influence price performance. Whether the stock price of a stock rises or falls, is subject to its own rules, which are sometimes difficult even for experts to see through.

Which factors determine the share price?

A stock exchange is a free market. This means that the price depends mainly on supply and demand. The more investors want to buy a particular stock, the higher the cost of the private capital. If there are more sellers than buyers, the price falls. But why, at some times, are there particularly many investors who are interested in a particular stock, and why do several shareholders simultaneously sell the same security?

Price fluctuations: why do share prices rise and fall?

More significant price fluctuations are often observed during AGMs, so when public companies present their annual results. Even though it is known that a company has received a large order, this news has a positive impact on price development. By contrast, financial scandals or legal proceedings against a well-known company cause the prices to fall as the value of the company decreases.

The art of a successful stock trader is to find the optimal time to buy a paper at a low price and profit from the subsequent price appreciation. Since buying a stock is a long-term investment, shoppers should not wait too long for the right price. Even though a higher price is paid for a stock, over the years, the issue often recovers from other profits and dividends paid.

Unlike cash deposits on a savings account or a savings account, no regular interest is paid on shares.

Nevertheless, equities are in a *well-stocked portfolio*, as investors call their portfolio. The purchase of shares is one of the long-term investment forms. Some shareholders retain their holdings for decades in the custody account. However, they must be aware that the share price is constantly changing, and the value of the securities may fall below the purchase price. If you sell your shares too fast when the price falls, you can suffer losses that can be avoided with sufficient patience. It's quite tricky.

Stocks as a pension

The purchase of shares is not suitable for a short-term investment. Dividends are usually distributed only once a year. Therefore, shares should be kept in the custody account, at least until the next dividend payment. Many investors buy shares for retirement or for long-term goals, such as educating children or purchase property as a retirement home. Equity funds, which invest many investors' money on the stock market, are also an alternative for acquiring individual stocks.

Shares or equity funds?

In addition to buying individual shares, numerous banks also offer equity funds and exchange-traded funds (ETFs). An equity fund collects the money of many investors and invests its inequities by the fund's guidelines. Many funds focus on individual sectors, conservative investments, companies from specific regions or countries, or securities with high potential returns. The fund shares are often offered from an investment of 25 euros, so this form of investment is also suitable for small investors. However, the return is not as high as buying individual stocks. This is because there are costs for managing the fund and the salary of the fund manager. To cover the expenses, the funds charge a sales charge, which the buyer has to pay.

ETF as an alternative

An alternative to traditional equity funds is an exchange-traded fund, abbreviated ETF. This fund is passively managed, so there are no high fees for a fund manager. Also, ETFs typically index. This results in a good diversification, as the diversification of the investment in different securities is called. Due to the diversified investment, losses of some papers are offset by the profits of other shares. Many ETFs show regular price increases. ETFs are often recommended for beginners who are currently entering the stock market because of lower fees and the high chance of a positive, high return.

Conditions for Trading in Equities

Beginners in stock trading must first acquire some knowledge about the process. To this end, serious advisers should be read, and the tips of well-known investors such as André Kostolany or Warren Buffet be respected. In addition to initial knowledge of the investment market, an investor must also have a custody account with a matching clearing account at his or her home bank or another bank. The purchased shares are kept in the custody account, from where they can also be resold.

Deposit account and clearing account

Many banks and savings banks offer a deposit account, often referred to as a deposit. The depot is not intended for daily payments. All securities held by an investor are recorded in the custody account. Accountants also need a clearing account to book transactions related to securities trading. This is either the checking account of the bank customer or, in some providers, even a money market account. Some banks offer free deposits, while other banks have custody account fees.

Deposit costs: Pay attention to the fees

Online banks, in particular, have free deposits in their offer, and also the billing account will not be charged any account management fees. Nevertheless, stock trading is not free. For every purchase and sale, there are order fees, which are different for each provider. Also, it may lead to the calculation of stock exchange fees and brokerage commissions. The amount of the fees investors know in the price-performance directory of the custodial bank. Also, the individual costs during the checkout are displayed.

As costs reduce returns, stock traders should compare the fees of different providers. The selection should also be paid attention to whether the bank has a free demo account on offer.

Free Demo Account

Some banks offer a free demo account that allows beginners to learn about stock trading. Account-holders will receive a virtual balance to buy any shares. The selected papers are not traded, but trading is only simulated. The price of the notional shares is adjusted to the current price fluctuations and changes regularly. The demo account allows beginners to learn different types of orders without risk and to try out investment strategies. For some providers, the offer of the free demo account is limited in time, while it is permanently available at other banks. A demo account is a perfect way to get to know the trade and understand the process for all those who enter the securities trading business.

Acting - online or in-person?

Stock traders who are well versed in stock exchange trading and do not need advice can independently trade through an online depository. After opening the account, the investor receives the access data for his custody account, including a clearing account. The order entry is online. Purchases and sales are executed immediately and posted to the accounts. As a rule, the providers of an online deposit require the lowest fees. Trading is possible on weekdays between 8:00 am and 10:00 pm for most online banks.

If you have questions about certain stocks or to buy, many banks offer orders by phone. Here answers either a voice computer or a consultant is directly on the phone. The calls are usually accepted only during bank opening hours. Besides, the fees for the telephone order acceptance are higher than in online trading.

If a trader maintains a custody account with a branch bank, he can also make an appointment with a trained securities advisor. The adviser provides comprehensive information on stock trading and issues an advisory report. Beginners will learn about the opportunities and risks of stock trading. Deposits at a branch bank, however, are usually more expensive due to the higher personnel costs, so it should be considered in advance whether personal contact with a bank account is essential or whether one can do without it.

Which stocks are suitable for beginners?

The 30 largest stock corporations are summarized in the Stock Index, abbreviated *DAX*. These include well-known names such as Adidas, BMW, Deutsche Bank, ThyssenKrupp, or Volkswagen. The DAX-listed brands are also known as *blue chips*. These are companies with a particularly high value. There are also blue-chip companies worldwide whose shares are listed in, for example, the American Dow Jones Index or the Japanese stock index Nikkei 225.

Beginners should first look at these stocks to minimize the risk of loss. As a rule, equities do not fluctuate too much. Therefore, investors can focus on other aspects of stock trading, such as the different order types. Often, the so-called index funds (ETFs) are recommended for beginners, as they are more cost-effective due to the automatic management and also have a high degree of diversification, which is why the price fluctuations are less.

How much money do I invest in stocks?

The most crucial tip when investing in stocks is that only money that is not needed in the short-term should be invested. Stock trading is a long-term investment. Therefore, the savings on the new car or vacation are not suitable for buying stocks.

Many investors choose to invest around 30% of their savings inequities. More important than the exact percentage of total assets, however, is a successful investment strategy that the investor should develop and stick to.

Under no circumstances should a loan be taken for trading in equities and other securities, as the risk of loss would lead to even more significant financial consequences. Invest only the money that you own and that you can forego in the longer term to get a high return.

Different Investment Strategies

One of the key tips from seasoned traders is that every investor should choose their investment strategy. This strategy should be maintained, even if stock prices are going in the wrong direction. To observe the development, the courses should be reviewed regularly. This does not have to be done daily. At least once a week, however, every investor should inform himself about the development of his portfolio.

Here is a list of the best-known investment strategies in stock trading:

- **Dividend strategy:** purchase of shares with high dividend payments.
- **Dividend growth strategy:** buy stocks with the highest dividends.
- **Momentum strategy:** buying stocks whose price has risen in the past and will continue to rise.
- **Reversal strategy:** buying stocks whose price has fallen and will increase again in the future.
- **Value strategy:** buying stocks below their value.
- **Index strategy:** Purchase of Exchange Traded Funds (ETF) that replicate an index.

Successful investors often combine multiple strategies to achieve the best return on trading stocks. The experts emphasize that an investor who trades in shares must also bear losses. This is also one of the biggest rookie mistakes: many inexperienced investors sell their holdings directly after the adverse price action has taken place. However, in such a situation, which is not uncommon, it is essential to keep a cool head and wait, rather than immediately resell.

Tips for Starting in Stock Trading

Every newcomer in stock trading must pay apprenticeship money and accept losses. But there are some tips on how to avoid typical rookie mistakes:

• *Patience pays off*

Patience is one of the most important virtues in stock trading. Price losses must not lead to panic sales but must be sustained. The savers should also note that every transaction is associated with costs. The fees for purchases and sales reduce the return and can even lead to a negative result.

• *Track-specific investment goals*

An investment in shares is not suitable for a quick profit. Successful investors have long been involved in the financial market and have also gained experience through short-selling. Therefore, an investor should not be too greedy but consistently pursue his investment objective. This includes critically questioning stories about supposedly quick profits of other stock traders and not following every trend.

• *Be informed about the stock market*

Newcomers to stock trading should familiarize themselves with the financial market and learn about some public companies. Experts advise dividing the fixed assets into different shares. Beginners should concentrate on fewer than ten stocks. Thus, the observation of the depot does not become too time-consuming. Also, the investor can react quickly to current economic news and market movements.

Investing in stocks is not suitable for every investor. However, anyone who acquires some knowledge about the stock market can make good profits with stock trading. Investors should invest money that they do not need urgently enough. Moreover, general interest in the financial market and patience are among the most important qualities of a successful trader. To make the first step towards successful securities trading, the book provides you with advanced topics such as the stock market, custody accounts, bonds, funds, ETFs, and leverage products sound information because knowledge is also the key to success in the financial world!

CHAPTER 8

SIMPLE STRATEGIES TO USE
Why use stock market strategies?

Here is a good question. Why is it worth using stock market strategies? You need to know that the financial instruments you are trading on, such as CFDs (contracts for difference), are already designed to be simplified and accessible for investment.

Even the platforms where you will find yourself performing from a practical point of view, your trading operations are very intuitive and can, therefore, be exploited both by industry experts who demand the possibility of trading professionally, via beginners who may never have put to this kind of tools but still want to create a monthly income by investing in the stock market.

One of the right reasons why it is worth learning the stock market strategies lies in the fact that we are sure that you too have always dreamed of finding a job that would not force you to move for long stretches, perhaps remaining stuck in traffic and city chaos, a job that does not oblige you to say yes to the boss on duty who may not even deserve to occupy that place, a job where you should not be forced to work overtime to be able to reach the end of the month charging you with stress and fatigue.

This is why we believe that trading with stock market strategies is the best possible alternative, not only offline but also online. Being independent in this promising world guarantees you the possibility to shake off the problems linked to the crisis to earn your freedom, even before the money, to become the master of your own life.

A thousand good reasons to trade with the right strategy

If you find yourself somehow, you have heard about the possibility of trading on the stock exchange, and maybe you know there is no way to do it online. If you want to take this path, we ask you not to feel intimidated or frightened by your possible future as a financial operator.

The stock exchange trading online has become a beginner or beginner's measure that it is. If, until today, you have only played lowly professions and do not have a higher degree, perhaps you think that you are not up to this kind of activity.

Perhaps you believe that the Stock Exchange and Markets, as well as the strategies to earn money, are beyond your means! Enough of this loser mentality.

The truth is that you are second to none, and you have the potential to be on a par with others and, why not, also to excel, especially in a world where meritocracy reigns like that of the stock market and financial markets on the internet.

Millions of people around the world have chosen the path of investment of their online capital, albeit very small. Now you can do it yourself by putting into practice the stock market strategies that we will propose to you during this guide.

Apply the right bag techniques

Do you think that all these people know every single nation and all the secrets of the financial markets to be able to earn a salary at the end of the month in this kind of activity?

This is not the case. Anyone who makes money from online trading does so from little to useful knowledge. It is, therefore, not a question of quantity; it is only a question of quality.

Few but good stock market strategies will allow you to become an established and successful trader who can afford to buy whatever he wants, in total independence, and without having to ask anyone for anything.

It is necessary to know as well as to apply the right bag technique. Learn it first through theory, then put it into practice in the field of trading, testing it continuously and optimizing it based on your trading methodology.

Do not miss the topics to come and immediately discover the best stock exchange strategies, the path that will lead you to become a real trader may be extended and tortuous, but in the end it will be worth it, and you will finally feel satisfied in an occupation free from conditioning and the harassment of the world of work as it has always known it.

If you start trading today, your old life will already be in the past, because you're about to be immersed in a virtuous circle of real opportunities to become an ace of stock trading. Cheers!

Difference Between Tactics And Stock Market Strategies

Modern stock exchange strategies have been devised to permanently change the old canons of traditional investment that made everything too slow and stiff, too challenging to apply, and this caused traders many problems and dissatisfactions, so much that many were eventually led to abandon this promising activity.

With the new strategies, the goal has been to make trading affordable and feasible for everyone, the doors are wide open, and anyone who wants it today can enter without suffering the typical problems of the past.

What it takes to make the most of the strategies that we propose to you in all respects is only basic knowledge of the subject of trading. Consequently, you are not called to know everything to start earning.

Therefore, trading does not mean having a degree in economics. After all, those who would be prepared today to face 5 years of studies to earn money, it is really too much time and too much sacrifice to put in place, so the techniques that you have to use to earn are simple but effective strategies that guarantee the success of the trades in most cases.

But because in stock trading, we talk about strategies and not tactics and because the former is much more successful and secure than the latter. The speech is very simple, and we want to clarify it with the following short definitions:

Investment Strategies

The strategy is the description of a long-term action plan used to set and subsequently coordinate all the actions that serve to achieve a particular, specific purpose. Strategies can be applied in all fields to reach the goal.

They, therefore, carry out the task of obtaining greater security by making a series of separate operations that help to reach an end goal. In the case of trading, we are talking about profit, which is undoubtedly the only primary aim that drives people to enter this business.

The simple tactic, on the other hand, is a course of action adopted according to the achievement of specific objectives, but in this case, we speak of small achievements in the short-term.

Adopting tactics would not be effective or satisfactory in the field of trading because it is not a structured plan, but simple plans to achieve small temporary objectives. In short, with a tactic you can also win a battle, but not war; winning a war requires a broader STRATEGY.

What all traders aim to achieve is a constant and lasting success over time that gives total security of a monthly income and specific collections on an annual basis. In stock exchange trading, it is possible to achieve all this by using strategies. Without strategies, you might perish as a trader very soon.

Applying stock exchange strategies requires attention and many precautions, especially at the beginning, when you are not much of an expert. In certain situations, when the markets become uncertain or careless, you do not know how to act, and you risk making mistakes.

At specific errors, however, the strategies cannot be remedied; in those cases, it will be the experience to act as a master and to suggest the right moves to make.

How much do you earn if you use the best strategy to invest?

With financial instruments available today, profit margins are simply impressive; operating in the right way, you can earn a lot of money even on a daily basis, but at that point, you have to take into account other factors such as the skill of the trader, the ability to avoid the losses, the amount of capital you have available, but also the small strokes of luck that from time to time can help to increase profits.

The amount of money that can be earned then also

depends, above all, on the financial product you intend to use. There are not very marked differences but still tangible, depending on whether you prefer to trade forex, CFD, or investing in social trading.

Stock Market Strategies And Money Management

If you intend to trade on the stock exchange, there is no doubt that you will, sooner or later, have to come into contact with the rules of money management or all that concerns the management of money and your precious investment capital.

Money Management shows you the way to correct money management, so it is fundamental in trading, but its rules are also applied in other fields that are as varied as in the domestic or business economy. Ultimately, the rules it dictates are quite simple and due to pure and simple common sense, but in any case, it will be necessary to observe them religiously to avoid running into severe problems in your career as a trader.

The creators of the first money management techniques had a clear idea that it was necessary to produce a new awareness of the use of money in their investments, for the first time imposing the concept of diversification and differentiation of the investment portfolio to reduce the risks of trading and losses on investment capital drastically.

A strategic approach to stock exchange trading cannot, therefore, ignore the knowledge of the fundamental precepts of money management that require you to always establish the spending limit and the budget available at the beginning.

In the field of trading, this will mean establishing the risks that you are willing to run within certain limits that not even an "Indiana Jones" of trading could ever think of crossing; otherwise, it would face economic suicide at the speed of light! The principles of money management help you put both the risks and the potential profits on the scales to understand if a particular movement on the markets should be exploited or not; in other words, it helps you to know if the game is worth the candle.

If you learn to put the rules of money management into practice, your long-term success can be practically assured, but even the short and medium-term will be more probable and easily accessible. In short, all this talk turns to a need for investment efficiency.

The best traders are those who can minimize losses, which not even the guru of the economy could ever avoid, and increase profits more and more.

The key to all this is precisely the fact that before learning to earn aspiring traders, the importance of learning to lose should be taught! Suffering losses and spilling money is a natural thing in trading, and you have to try to understand it and not give too much weight when a loss occurs.

The main rule of money management states that you should never, never, ever put at risk more than 5% of the total capital available in single trading operation.

Doing so would be stupid because it means that in case of loss, you should lose a lot of time trying to recover the negative position if you succeed. Furthermore, it is necessary to avoid losing more than 30% of the total capital available in a single trading day.

You simply have to recognize that when a bad day happens, you have to have the courage to turn off the computer or the device that you used to use to go for a nice walk and not run any further risk because it is clear that that day or you are not able to operate correctly or things in some way always row against you. It is the case to abandon the current session as soon as possible.

Best Strategies For Investing

In the following list, we present the best stock market strategies that you can use to succeed as a trader in the financial markets. Let's talk about very effective trading techniques to exploit with.

• *Adx Strategy*

The first strategy to which we want to introduce you is that which is based on the Adx, a very special but at the same time, easy to read trading indicator. This indicator has a rather intriguing history because initially, it was used for analysis only on the raw materials market, and later on, its inventor, Welles Wilder, decided to test it also on other markets immediately realizing its incredible potential.

If the markets are based on trend analysis, the ADX is the right indicator to find them and measure their strength. This strategy will be very suitable to find the best trends and exploit them to your advantage, increasing profits and always having the pulse of the situation under control.

• *The Cage Strategy*

This instead is a somewhat atypical stock exchange strategy and different from the others but equally valid and also very special to use and implement. Both beginners and professionals adopt it for its simplicity. The elements you need to make the most of the strategy are few.

CHAPTER 9

THE PARAMETERS TO CONSIDER

Operators use technical analysis to help them better understand what is happening in the market and gain a potential perspective of what can happen next. Many operators, who are new to technical analysis, often have misconceptions about what it is and what it is not and what you can do for them. There are five essential aspects of technical analysis that can, if better understood, help traders better determine entry and exit points, as well as offer clues about the possible future direction of the price.

1. All information is discounted in the price.

Fundamental analysts focus on things like earnings and sales figures to determine the appropriate "value" for a given stock. A technical analyst is less interested in "why" an action or asset is traded at a specific price, and more interested in "where" it can go next. In essence, a technical analyst believes that all the good and bad "news" related to the market or assets are already reflected in the price information.

2. The volume can offer important information.

Many price movements, such as breaking to a new high, for example, are generally considered of greater importance if they are accompanied by a higher than average volume of operations. For most technical analysts, the higher the trading volume, the more "valid" the break is typically considered since a large volume means great conviction and enthusiasm from operators. This is why the volume appears in the chart of all technical operators before any other indicator or tool.

3. Markets are driven by psychological factors, in addition to the fundamental ones.

The demand for a given value increases or decreases depending on the collective assessment that all traders perform concerning the real or perceived value of that value. For example, an announcement about strong sales and profit growth for a given company can make traders have a more favorable opinion regarding the shares of that company. As a result, the company's stock demand may increase. A technical analyst will try to identify this by recognizing the improvement in the price action and the increase in the volume of operations.

4. Prices tend to move in trends and patterns.

Public perceptions can change quickly. Sometimes, these changes affect perceptions about the stock market in general, or broader financial markets in general. Other times, these changes affect only a particular segment of the market or a specific stock. However, most of the time, the price of many assets moves actively without any concomitant "news" that can explain "why" this movement is occurring. This often makes it appear that price movements are random. However, experience has shown that price action often falls into patterns and "trends."

A "trend" can be defined as the general direction of a given price for a given time. It is assumed that a trend will be in effect until a clear signal is given that that particular trend has been reversed.

Types of trends:

There are three different types of trends: bullish, bearish, and lateral.

- *Bull Trend*

An upward trend is defined as a series of higher lows and higher highs over a given period of time. Connecting these rising lows with a trend line is a standard technical analysis tool that can help identify whether an uptrend is intact or not.

- *Downward Trend*

A downtrend is defined as a series of lower highs and lows. Connecting these high decreasing points with a trend line is a standard technical analysis tool that can help identify whether a downtrend is intact or not.

- *Lateral trend*

A lateral tendency is a series of ups and downs within a relatively flat or compressed range. Connecting these high and low points with a couple of trend lines can help identify the trading range. A standard tool of many technical analysts is to look for breakdowns above or below a defined trading range to indicate when a new uptrend or downtrend can begin.

The Timeframe Of The Trend

The time frame of the trend can play a vital role for many traders. Price trends can last days, weeks, months, years, or just a few minutes. It is essential to consider which period of time is the most important for your negotiation style. The longer a given trend persists, the higher it's meaning. In general, it is believed that the longer the period of time, the stronger and more useful the signals that are generated. For an intraday analysis, the trend with 1-minute bar graphs may be significant. For virtually all analysis time frames, minute-by-minute price changes are not substantial. The duration of the trend is divided into three-time frames:

- ## Primary Trend
  - This category includes trends that last from six months to several years.
- ## Secondary Or Intermediate Trend.
  - This category generally includes trends that last from one to six months.
- ## Minor Or Short-Term Trend.
  - This trend category usually lasts from one day to a couple of weeks.

Remember: "The trend is your friend."

Because the concepts of trends are so fundamental to technical analysis, many traders have a saying about "the trend is their friend." This adage suggests that operators take advantage of the primary prevailing trend, rather than operating against, or "fighting" that.

5. Work to increase your weight of evidence, not to find the Holy Grail

Trading signals can provide operators with a clear set of criteria to search and help them better identify possible opportunities. However, using only a technical analysis tool or an indicator only gives you a fraction of the image of what is happening with the market or the asset. On the other hand, the use of too many indicators can result in an operator feeling overwhelmed or having "analysis paralysis" because of the number and, sometimes, the exchange signals, in conflict.

Many operators look for signs of a combination of only a few tools and indicators to build their "weight of evidence" to help them make more objective and less emotional decisions instead of reacting to any price movement in a reactionary manner.

No technical tool or indicator will have a perfect signal register. There will always be the possibility of false or conflicting signals. Nor is there a specific number or combination of tools or indicators that work for everyone.

That is why it is essential to identify some clear trading signals that you understand and that best adapt to the trading strategy.

What's Next

It is an excellent idea to examine more closely the technical analysis tools that are of interest to you. Doing this can help you better understand how each tool works, so you can determine the best way to adapt to your trading strategy and plan.

CHAPTER 10

START WITH THE SIMULATOR

Investing in the stock market, as the experts point out, requires substantial knowledge and experience to control the risk and make the appropriate decisions at the right time. That is why a *virtual stock market simulator* can become a fundamental tool to start trading with securities eliminating the dangers one can't afford much with one's hard-earned capital.

These simulators generally offer very advanced interfaces, a virtual economic fund to invest, and real-time information. That is to say; they have all the tools and functions necessary to learn how to invest in an online stock market as if we were in the stock market itself.

Many of these computer programs belong to banks and brokers specialized in the stock market or markets such as Forex (such as Plus500). These applications, from our point of view, are more complete than the simple stock market games that we have found in the market for decades or than the apps that have overwhelmingly increased in recent years.

In this chapter, we are going to analyze five exciting simulators for beginners, so that you can get valuable experience in a virtual stock exchange system before giving way to the real world. Most offer free demo accounts, although in some cases, we can find companies that request a small payment in exchange for using their platform. A small expense that is worth taking on, and that can save us many dislikes in the future.

Why Use A Bag Simulator?

Investing in the stock market is not especially difficult, but it is essential to have good knowledge to avoid greater evils. If you want to achieve high profitability, you have to take risks, but doing it blindly can be a real disaster for our pocket. It can be suicidal, financially speaking.

That is why it is essential to train previously in everything related to the markets and their operation. For this, you can go to the editorial fund of the National Commission of the Stock Market or the Madrid Stock Exchange, where we can find practical guides and handy tips for beginners and more advanced investors.

Having the advice of an expert is also a guarantee, but if you prefer to take the road alone, we recommend that you settle the bases well before playing with real money. The risk, as we have repeated, is high if it is operated without the necessary knowledge. The stock market is not a lottery that can make you rich by investing a few euros, so you should know all the mechanisms of the market entirely to understand *where* and *when* to put your money.

In this learning process, a good stock market simulator plays an essential role. With these tools, you can play with fictitious money, see how your decisions affect your income statement, and, most importantly, create solid pillars to leap to the real world of investments.

Another advantage is that the companies that offer these simulators allow you to directly operate with real money from the same or similar platform, so you will already be familiar with the interface. In many cases, it is only necessary to convert your demo account into a real account and make an income, without changing the program.

Pay for a bag simulator?

Many people are wondering what the best free bag simulator for beginners is. It is true that in the market, we can find compelling tools that do not require the payment of any amount, but it is also true that skimping on this section can be a real mistake.

Creating a CFD bag simulator that offers guarantees entails a considerable programming expense and high operating costs. That is why some companies ask for a small subscription in exchange for their use that does not usually reach 10 euros per month. A minimum amount for a tool that tells you how to learn to invest in the stock market from home and that allows you to practice with all the guarantees; it's worth it by any standards, of course.

Also, it is widespread that with that small fee, the user has access to manuals, tutorials, webinars, and other teaching materials to support the practical part with theoretical foundations. Investing in the stock market in the short term is not recommended, so all this material can be of high relevance to fix concepts.

The Best Bag Simulators

Once this preamble has been completed, we will analyze five of the most exciting simulators in the market. All are backed by companies with ample experience in the sector (they are banks or brokers) and are well above in quality and performance of simple stock games (we do not recommend using these games as part of your training). This listing is sorted alphabetically.

- *Active Trade*

This real-time stock market simulator offers users an account with 100,000 virtual euros so they can practice without fear of losing their money. It has personalized support and, most importantly, with courses and trading programs taught by professional traders.

With this tool, you can create your strategy, control your investments, find the companies that best fit your profile, and get detailed information on more than 18,400 shares. Essential functions to create your profile as an investor and locate those opportunities that you can take advantage of in the real world.

- *IG Spain*

The demo account of this stock market simulator allows

you to invest in an online stock market in a risk-free environment. This free account has a virtual fund of 20,000 euros and offers graphics and prices in real-time. Also, you can check from your mobile or tablet to continue operating anywhere, even if you don't have a computer. The interface can be customized to suit your tastes and your style.

This demo account, however, does not offer all the functionality of the real platform. The most notable differences are the following:

- Transactions made through the demo account are not subject to slippage, interest or dividend adjustments, or price movements out of the negotiation.
- Transactions can be rejected if you do not have enough funds to open them, but they will not be denied due to size or price issues.
- The graphics packages have no cost.
- The positions will not be closed if you do not have enough funds to cover the margin or current losses, something that does happen in a real account.

- *Orey iTrade*

Another easy-to-use bag simulator is that of Orey iTrade. With this tool, you will learn to invest in both the Spanish selective, that is, in the IBEX 35, as in other critical global exchanges. All online and free, since you can try it without cost and obligation.

Through its interface, you can access stock quotes in real-time and different analyses, comparative, and graphical tools. The account begins with a virtual fund of 100,000 euros to start investing.

- ## *Société Générale*

This trading simulator seems to us one of the most interesting since it will allow you to delve into the world of warrants, something that is not available in most of the free tools. The simulator of this French bank makes available to its users 10,000 fictitious euros to negotiate on the listed products of Société Générale and test their investment strategy without risk.

To start operating, you must register on the website www.sgbolsa.es. Registration is free. Also, the entity usually raffles gifts such as mobile phones or tablets among its new users, one more argument to try the Market Simulator, as they call it.

To use the system, follow these steps:

- Register on the website www.Warrants.com.
- Connect to the website www.Warrants.com or the simulator using the e-mail and the registration password.
- Access the simulator from the Tools menu of the website www.Warrants.com.

- ## Tradertwit

The Tradertwit simulator catches our attention since it has enormous educational value. It is not free (although it is cheap), but instead offers training and a compelling platform. They have a lot of news from the sector, an exciting collaborative platform, and thousands of interactive analyses.

We like what they call *"the challenge."* It is something like a 50-level training program that puts users in challenges to move from level to level. In each of them, you have to follow instructions, such as the maximum lever that can be used or the maximum loss streak. There are also objectives to be achieved.

Based on these criteria, the user can carry out operations of buying and selling currencies, indices, or raw materials — an excellent way to learn while having fun and competing against other users in the community. Also, the best usually takes real prizes.

CHAPTER 11

THE MOST COMMON QUESTIONS ABOUT TRADING

1. Can you live on trading?

Yes, just as you can live from medicine, from being a teacher, from being an architect, engineer, or lawyer. You require the same weapons: education, training, practice, guidance, discipline, perseverance, and a lot of determination to be a great professional in your field. Trading is no different. Perhaps many people have been wrong to think that when opening an account in a broker, funding their accounts, and starting trading means having the results to live from trading in less than what a rooster sings and being millionaires. Very wrong!!! It's like pretending to be a surgeon overnight. If you can live from trading, the question is, do you have what it takes to do it and achieve it?

2. What do I do to start trading?

The first and most important thing is to educate yourself about what trading is and how to do it effectively. Start by knowing the nature of trading, what it is about, how you win, who participates, how is the market that has been chosen, etc., are some of the things you should keep in mind. Don't get to war empty-handed. Go prepared. How? Find someone to inspire you, to teach these things, to

135

guide you, invest money and time in your education. There are many online trading schools, and you can be overwhelmed at first by searching, but choose the one that has a simple system, that its philosophy resonates with you, and that has your feet set on the ground. Avoid those that promote phrases like "fast millionaire trading in the Stock Exchange," "trading is straightforward," etc. You have to be realistic, and a school that tells you from the beginning what is trading, how it works, how it is earned, how it is lost and that it is not as easy as many want to make it believe in profiting, is a school that is worth considering.

3. When will I start seeing results?

When you have firmly rooted in a simple trading system, faithfully and disciplined, fulfilling your trading plan and adequately managing the risk-benefit, paradoxically, you will also begin to see the results when you detach yourself from the results and focus on the process. The process of trading involves the observation and reflection of our performance, the emotions experienced, the most frequent mistakes and annihilation, the analysis of the logbook, and the correction of the things that you can change and improve. You will begin to see results when, in addition to all these things, you continue working on your mind without giving up.

4. How much money can I start trading, and what broker should I use?

It depends on each broker and the instrument you use. If you want to trade stock options in Thinkorswim, for example, you will need at least $ 2,000 to access the options. If you're going to trade with stocks, you will need $ 25,000. With the other brokers, it will be different. On the website of the brokers are the most frequent questions and customer service that can take you from all doubts regarding minimum money to start, documents such as funds and how to remove, etc. Find the broker that is regulated, that has a good reputation, that other people are using and tell you about their experience.

5. How much money per month can I generate by trading?

The one that allows you the size of your account and the amount you are going to invest per operation, as long as you have the capabilities required to make money consistently. This brings us to question # 1. It's that easy.

6. How to achieve consistency?

Consistency is achieved by having consistent behaviors and actions. That is, if I have planned trading that tells me what it looks like an opportunity, where to go, where to place the stop, how to manage and how to manage risk, and do it over and over again which tells me that plan consistently then I'll have consistent results. But if you change the policy, each has a stop or every time you have a losing streak then you will go into an endless loop in which as emotional and impatient trader will modify or change it again and again, the plan and the results will be different. This is what happens to 95% who lose money doing trading; there is no clear, defined, and precise plan to follow consistently, disciplined, and with a lot of confidence.

7. What is the best strategy or trading system?

The one that is simple to understand, that you can even explain it to a child and the child understands it. Stay away from those systems that require more than five different indicators, that your attention away from price action scribbles filling your screen and does not have proper management of risk-benefit. The best strategy or system is simple, clear, proven (functional), and above all, fits your personality and type of trader. The method of a trader may not be the system that suits you; for that reason, you must define what type of trader you are if you are scalper, intraday or swing, and of course, your risk tolerance (conservative or risky). These are just a few things to consider when choosing a trading system.

8. I have lost much of my capital; what do I do?

If you have lost a large part of your capital, it is because you do not have a clear, defined and proven trading plan, there are no consistent behaviors that lead to consistent results; emotions dominate you, and there is also no proper risk-benefit management. In that sentence is the answer to this question. What you should do is simple: make a clear trading plan with a clear and straightforward strategy, try it in a demo, manage risk-benefit properly, trust 100% in your plan, work on your emotions being aware of them before, during and after of operations, record, and evaluate to be able to learn from your failures.

If the results are positive, return to real account and repeat the process focusing your attention on the emotions you experience and your reactions.

9. What actions do you recommend operating to start?

I recommend trading stocks that do not have a widespread, that are not very volatile and offer economic contracts near ITM. These are terms that you may not understand if you are starting. Once you know what the ideal requirements are, go to the Finviz map of actions and look for the best-known actions in each sector, write them down, go to your platform and look at their contract and spread grid, so you are choosing and removing from the list until have your ideal portfolio of at least 6 shares.

10. I have no time to trading regularly, what are my options?

You can choose to do swing trading. The swing will allow you to open an operation today and close it several days later. You will need a trading system that suits this style, have your stop defined so that it protects your capital while you are away, and periodically review operations. Some brokers have mobile applications that allow you to monitor operations from your cell phone. If the situation is that you cannot trade in the morning, you can choose to make a trading plan for the afternoon hours, and it will work the same.

CONCLUSION:

The fear of losing in online trading

Among the most severe and frequent psychological risks that a trader can run, there is undoubtedly one of ending up crushed by the dangers of "loss aversion." That is, the fear of losing could excessively limit the trader's ability to act, leading him to bring him back into a condition of extreme prudence that could throw off any strategic plan.

It is known that traders who fear losses are much more likely to maintain their losing positions, for example, than traders who can accept short-term losses and move on to more profitable transactions. Maintaining the positions at a loss, without respecting your strategy plan, is a serious mistake, as it jeopardizes the stability of your portfolio, not only by accumulating negative results but also, and above all, by preventing capital from being profitably used for better operations.

But how to know if you are afraid of losses? If you want to see if you have any tendency to lose to aversion or not, ask yourself if you have ever been inside a losing trade beyond the point where you knew you would have to go out. Behavior that you may have held because you hoped that the financial instrument on which you have bet would have reversed its course from unfavorable to positive, eliminating the losses accrued.

141

If the answer is definite, you must immediately become aware of the fact that you are "victims" of an excessive aversion to losses. Therefore, you must become aware of these characteristics and directly ask yourself how to overcome loss aversion quickly and effectively!

Well, in this sense, the best way to overcome a loss aversion prejudice is to operate with stop-loss orders set at the opening of the position and managed automatically by your broker. Many traders claim to have the habit of operating with a "mental" stop-loss, that is, with a stop loss level at which they think and promise to act if the financial instrument touches that level. However, too often, traders fail to act on their mental stop losses. So they let their emotions get in the way and start to rationalize their choice to stay in the trade until they think it will turn their direction upside down.

Conversely, as soon as you enter a position, set your stop-loss order with the broker, in such a way as to wipe out the emotions at this juncture.

Excessive Self-Confidence

Forex traders have to compete not only with other traders in the forex market but also with themselves. Often, as a Forex trader, you will be your worst enemy yourself! On the other hand, as human beings, we are naturally emotional. Our ego wants to be validated - we want to prove to ourselves that we know what we are doing, and we can take care of ourselves. And we also have a natural survival instinct!

All of these emotions and instincts can be combined to provide us with particularly essential successes. However, most of the time, our emotions will prevail and lead to losses, unless we learn to control them.

Many Forex traders believe it would be ideal if you could completely separate yourself from your emotions. Unfortunately, this is almost impossible. Moreover, it must be remembered that some of your emotions will help you improve your trading success. The best thing you can do for yourself is to learn to understand yourself and pay attention to specific elements. For example, do you know how to manage excessive self-confidence?

Overconfidence is exaggerated esteem in their Forex trader capacity. If you find yourself thinking of yourself as someone who has understood everything, who has nothing more to learn... then you are probably suffering from an *excess* of trust and confidence in yourself—not conducive at all!

Traders who are too self-confident tend to get in trouble by trading too often or placing significant transactions, trying to cash out as much as possible. Inevitably, an over-confident trader will end up trading unwisely and unreasonably, risking too much on the only operation that goes wrong and quickly running out of his account.

The best way to overcome the prejudice of excessive trust is to establish a rigorous set of risk-management rules. These rules should at least cover how many positions you should open and manage at one time, how much of your account you are willing to risk on a single transaction, and how much of your account you are ready to lose before taking a break from trading and re-evaluating your strategy.

Be The Master Of Your Own Life

Happy Trading

www.ingramcontent.com/pod-product-compliance
Lightning Source LLC
Chambersburg PA
CBHW071701210326

41597CB00017B/2277